DATE DUE

MAR 3 1 1997	
APR 2 3 1997	

elementary fashion design and trade sketching

elementary fashion design and trade sketching

second edition

written and illustrated by
MAXINE WESTERMAN

FAIRCHILD PUBLICATIONS • NEW YORK

Second Printing 1975
Third Printing 1977

Standard Book Number: 87005-438-4

Library of Congress Catalog Card Number: 82-083389

Printed in the United States of America

contents

introduction

This workbook is essentially a primary course of study for the would-be-designer, presenting a step-by-step approach to the business of designing apparel.

Its purpose is twofold:

1. How to create original dress designs, starting with the most basic styles and progressing towards the more complex.
2. How to demonstrate these original designs on paper in a simple, attractive manner. This is achieved by providing the student (who may or may not be able to draw) with the tools for self expression. Such a tool is the *croqui* or undressed fashion figure. The finished illustration which makes use of a croqui is called a *trade sketch,* because it is used in the fashion trade or industry.

To derive the best results from this course of study, the work for each unit should be done in the order of its presentation. Assignments (or lessons) are carefully planned to provide maximum growth through a series of slow and steady progressions. But the degree of individual success achieved will depend greatly upon the amount of time and energy devoted to assignments, and the accuracy with which instructions are followed.

UNIT 1
a list of supplies

a list of supplies

It is practically essential that work begins with the proper tools. While substitutes are available for the supplies listed below, none will assure the same quality results.

A FEW NUMBER 2H DRAWING PENCILS— Drawing pencils are usually made of different qualities of lead, either hard or soft. Soft leads are designated by the letter "B" and hard leads by the letter "H." The higher the number the softer the lead in the "B" pencils, and the higher the number the harder the lead in the "H" pencils.

A "2H" pencil is just hard enough to draw a crisp, clear line which doesn't smear, and soft enough to achieve the variety of accent required for fashion sketching.

A KNEADED ERASER—Kneaded erasers are gray in color and can be stretched and pulled, somewhat like chewing gum. They leave no marks or debris, and are therefore excellent for cleaning smudges, as well as for most other general pencil work.

A SMALL, PORTABLE PENCIL SHARPENER— Any sharpener which adequately sharpens pencils will do. Very sharp lines are particularly important for detailed work.

A DRAWING BOARD—Drawing boards are rectangular pieces of pine or some other soft wood. They vary in size, but the most popular are about 18" x 24". A piece of masonite may be substituted for a drawing board. Masonite, a type of board used in the construction industry, is thin, hard, or lighter weight than the typical drawing board, and considerably less expensive.

PUSH PINS AND/OR MASKING TAPE—Push pins function like thumbtacks, but they have bigger heads and longer, thinner points. Used for securing drawing paper and other loose work to the drawing board, they prevent slipping and leave no noticeable holes in the wood. If masonite is used instead of the regular drawing board, then push pins *cannot* be used because masonite is too hard. In that case, substitute *masking tape* for push pins. Masking tape will secure your paper to the masonite board and can be used over and over again without tearing or damaging your paper. (Masking tape will also be used for some of the exercises in this book.)

TRACING PAPER—Tracing paper is a thin, transparent paper required for every project in this workbook. It is available in pads or by the package. The recommended size is 9" x 12".

The following supplies are not needed until you study Unit 9.

VELLUM PAPER—Vellum is somewhat thicker and slightly less transparent than tracing paper. It is sometimes called "heavy tracing paper" and is used for finished color illustrations. The techniques of coloring on vellum, discussed in Units 9 and 11, are the same as those used in many manufacturers' showrooms.

A BOX OF COLORED DRAWING PENCILS— Colored drawing pencils are used for finished color illustrations on vellum. The best assortment will have a variety of colors, including at least two values of a particular color. For example, a light blue and a darker blue, a light green and a darker green, and so on.

A CAN OF FIXATIVE SPRAY—Fixative, sprayed on a piece of finished artwork, leaves an invisible protective coating which prevents pencil work from smudging, and ensures a clean, professional appearance.

All of the above supplies will be available at art supply stores. Some, such as 2H pencils, kneaded erasers, and pencil sharpeners, may also be purchased in stationery shops. Drawing boards and masonite boards are usually obtained at art supply stores, but may be purchased less expensively from a lumberyard.

UNIT 2 what makes good design?

LESSON ONE

SOME GENERAL PRINCIPLES

- Proportion
- Unity
- Repetition
- A Point of Interest
- Economy of Design Motifs

LESSON TWO

THE EFFECT OF STYLE LINES ON APPEARANCE

- Horizontal Lines
- Vertical Lines
- Placement of the Waistline
- Shape or Silhouette
- Length of Skirt

LESSON ONE

some general principles

The great names of fashion achieved their fame because instinctive genius, in addition to a great store of knowledge and experience, enabled them to know precisely what or what not to do in the course of their designing. They required few rules to guide them.

As a beginning student, however, without the benefit of years of experience—years of looking at and feeling fashion—you may find it helpful to refer to some general principles of good design. These are not rules to be strictly adhered to, but rather are ideas which may offer guidance to the novice.

PROPORTION

The size of one part of a garment in relation to its other parts is referred to as *proportion*. For example, a sleeve which is so large that it overwhelms the rest of a dress is out of proportion, or disproportionate. Part of an outfit which is too small may also be disproportionate.

One part of each of the garments in Figures 3, 4, and 5, is out of proportion. Can you tell what they are?

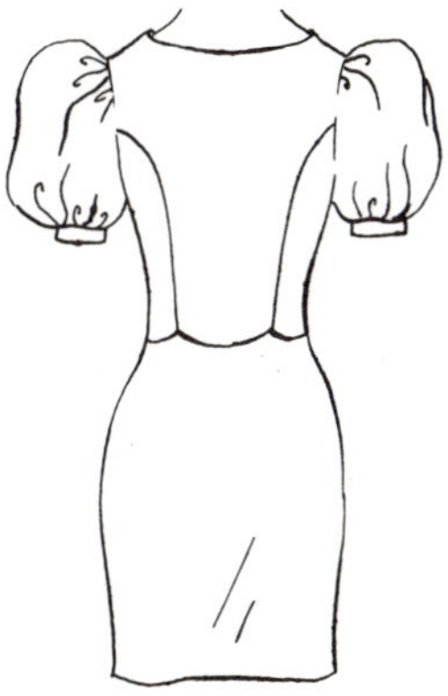

Figure 1.
Out of Proportion
Sleeves are too large for size of skirt.

Figure 2.
In Proportion
Sleeves are balanced by a longer skirt.

Figure 3

Figure 4

Figure 5

UNITY

When a costume, or for that matter any work of art—a painting or a piece of music—has *unity*, the separate and individual parts work together to create a whole. There is a feeling of togetherness, of oneness. The dress in Figure 6 lacks unity. The tailored look in the skirt is incongruous with the fluffiness of the top. Unity is achieved in Figure 7 by carrying the design motif* (in this case stitching) up into a simplified top.

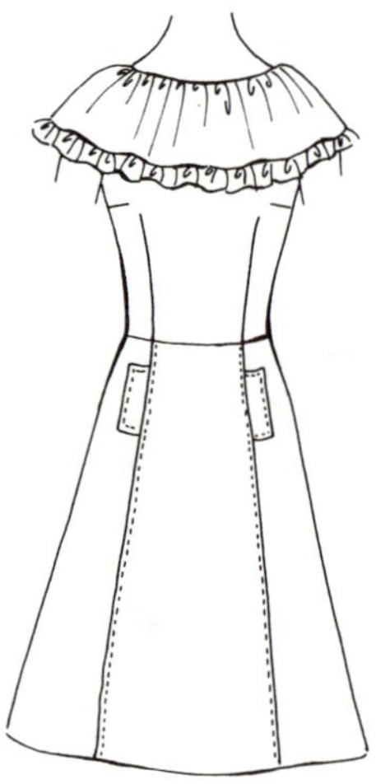

Figure 6.
No unity

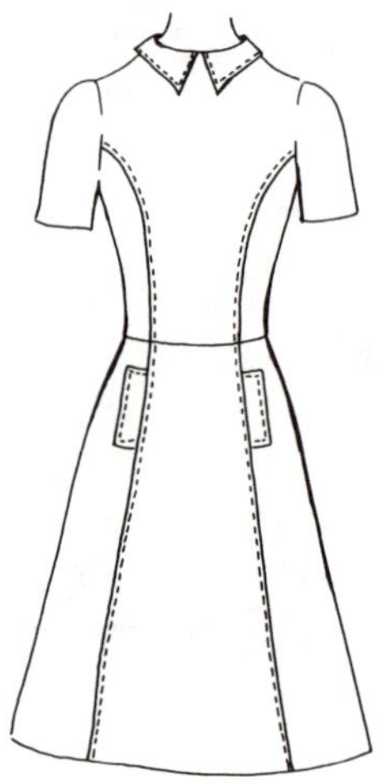

Figure 7.
Unity

REPETITION

The repetition of a design element (motif) throughout a garment will create a sense of unity. Conversely, the use of too many motifs in one costume is distracting, discordant. The simple and tasteful designs of the dresses illustrated in Figures 8, 9, and 10 are based completely upon the repetition of motifs.

Figure 8.
Curved shapes
are repeated.

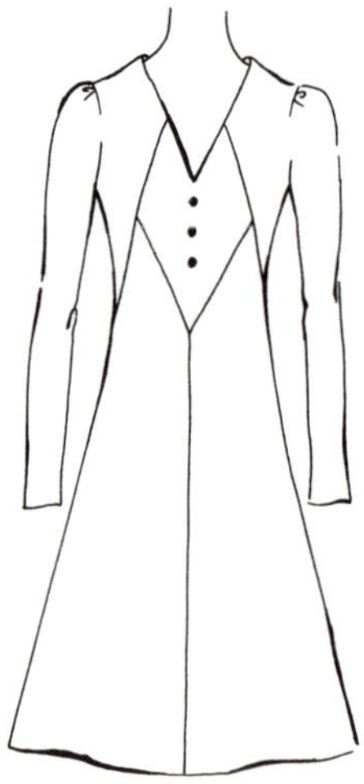

Figure 9.
V-shapes
are repeated.

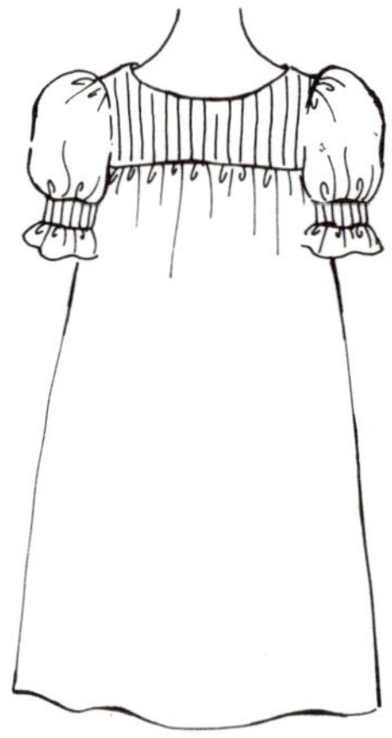

Figure 10.
Tucks and shirring
are both repeated.

*The word "motif" will be used throughout this workbook to mean a design idea or element. For example, stitching, shirring, the shape of a seamline, a color—all are design ideas, elements, or motifs.

A POINT OF INTEREST

Many clothes are not reliant upon the repetition of motifs for good design. Their attraction is based instead upon the dominance of only one design element—*the point of interest.* A point of interest is that place on an outfit that catches and holds your attention.

If, however, there is more than one major point of interest, the result is distracting. When a garment is designed so that a strong focus of interest is the main attraction, the other parts must be subordinate to that dominant area.

The dresses illustrated in Figures 13 and 14 are poorly designed. Each has more than one point of interest. How would you improve them?

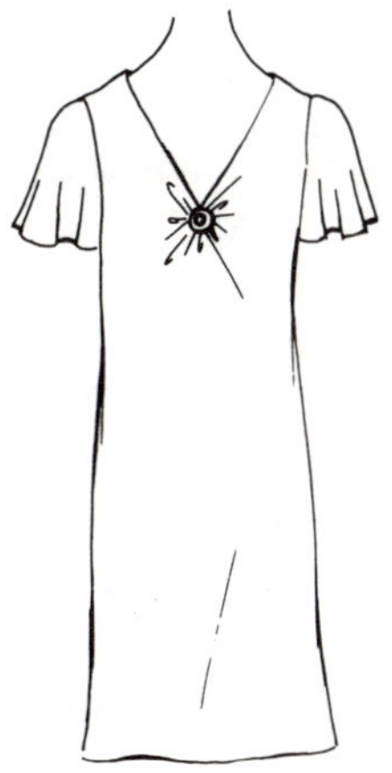

Figure 11

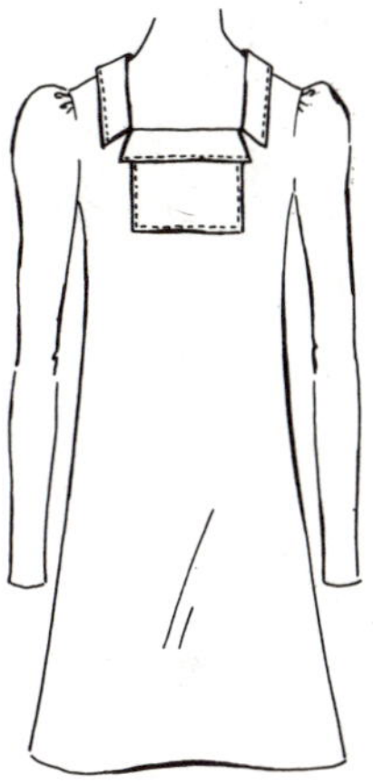

Figure 12

Figure 13

Figure 14

ECONOMY OF DESIGN MOTIFS

Being economical with the use of design motifs refers to limiting the number of ideas introduced in one costume.

Figures 15 and 16 illustrate the use of too many design elements, such as ruffles, flares, buttons, trimming, a bow, stitching, seaming, pockets, pleats, and a collar detail.

Figures 17 and 18 have been simplified. Excessive elements have been removed, thereby economizing on the number of design motifs.

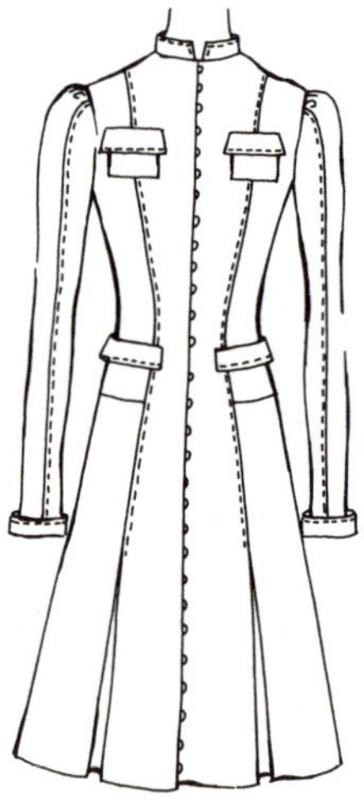

Figure 15

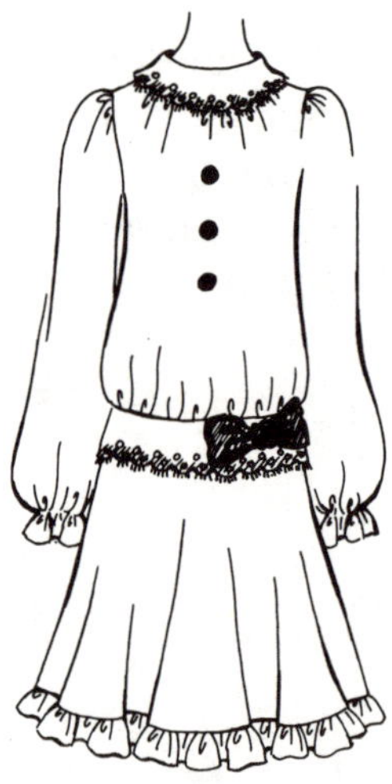

Figure 16

Figure 17

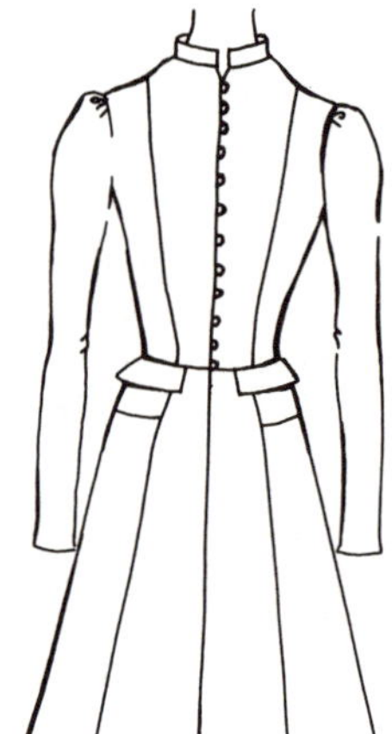

Figure 18

LESSON TWO

the effect of style lines on appearance

The style lines of a costume can make the wearer appear taller, shorter, fatter, or thinner than she really is. Optical illusions may thus be intentionally created by clever designers who know how and where to place style lines.

Horizontal lines (those which move across) add width to the figure, while *vertical* lines (those which move up and down) add height.

In addition to the effects created by the use of horizontal or vertical lines, *the placement of the waistline, the shape or silhouette of a garment,* and *the length of the skirt* also create eyefooling effects.

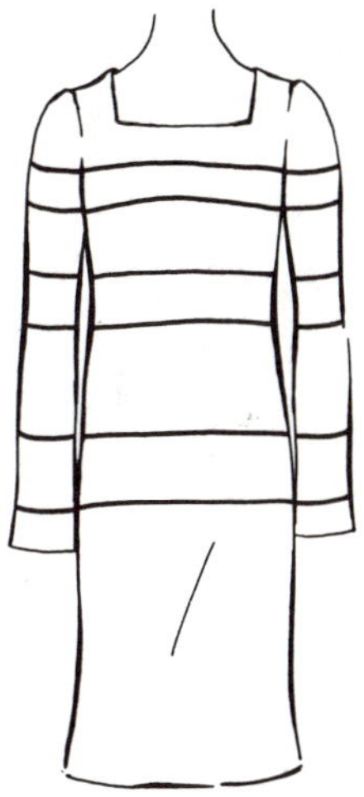

Figure 19.
Horizontal style lines

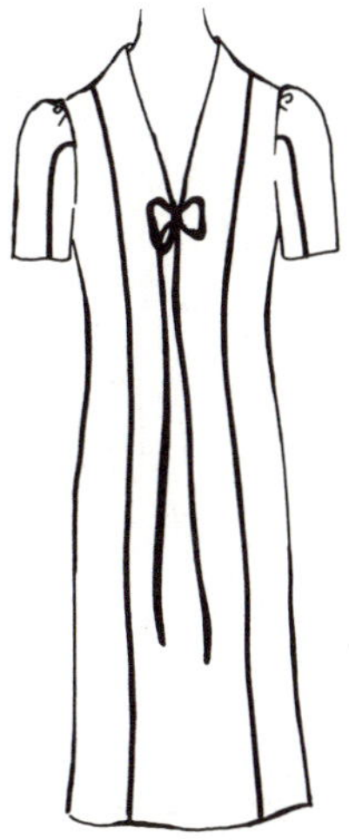

Figure 20.
Vertical style lines

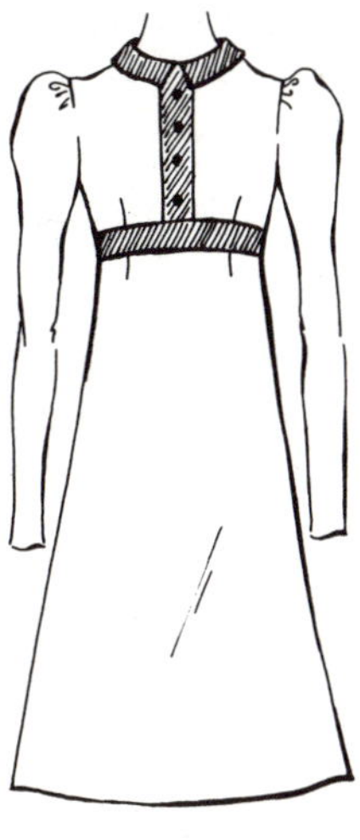

Figure 21.
High waistline makes figure appear taller.

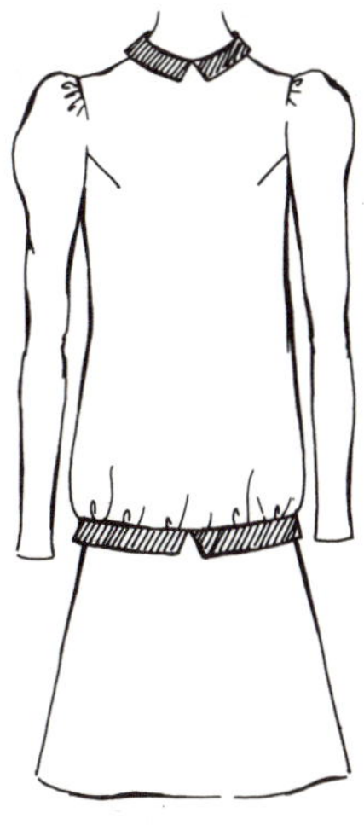

Figure 22.
Low waistline makes figure appear shorter.

Figure 23.
Fitted top and A-line skirt
make figure appear slimmer.

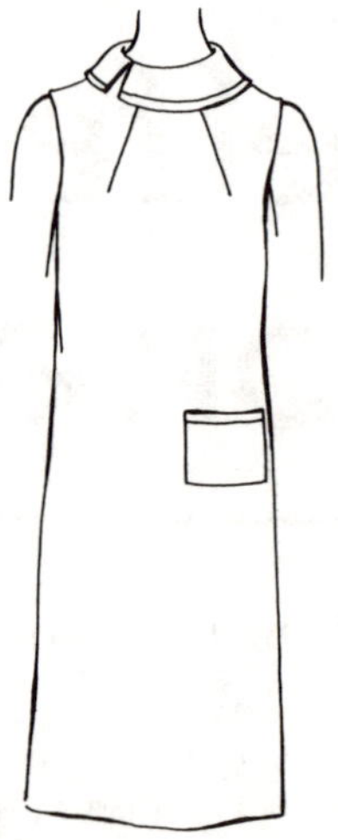

Figure 24.
Shift silhouette minimizes
body shape.

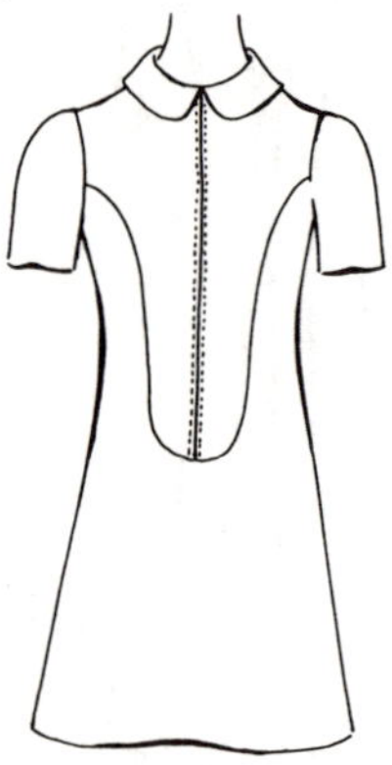

Figure 25.
Short skirt makes
figure appear shorter.

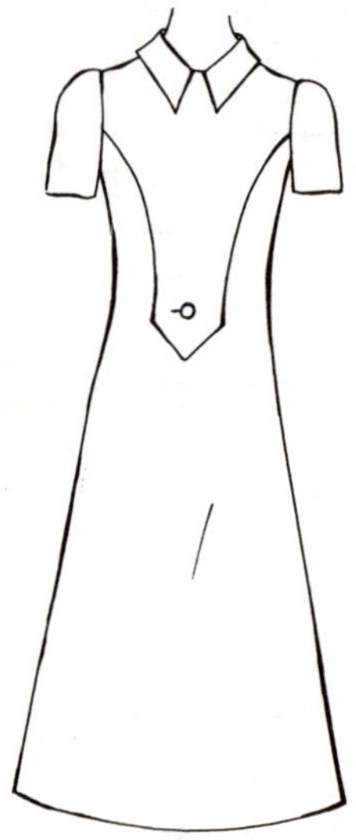

Figure 26.
Long shirt makes
figure appear longer.

UNIT 3
sources of inspiration for design

LESSON THREE

HISTORICAL AND CONTEMPORARY SOURCES

LESSON FOUR

TRIMMING AND FABRIC

LESSON THREE

historical and contemporary sources

HISTORICAL SOURCES

Historical costumes are an excellent source of inspiration for design. The best place to research them is at a local public library. Any book on the history of costume will provide a treasure of design ideas at your disposal. They may also be found on television and in movies, old newspapers, photographs and magazines, history books, museums and paintings.

How do we employ costumes for our own designing purposes? Do we copy, or do we adapt? Used intelligently, material such as this stimulates creative thinking because it provides the designer with hundreds of design elements which may then be adapted in completely new and original ways.

The suit designs in Figures 2 and 3 were both inspired by the dress in Figure 1. The pleated shoulder detail in Figure 2 can be traced directly to the ruffled capelet in the costume. The source of inspiration for Figure 3 is not so obvious. Can you find the detail that was adapted from Figure 1?

Figure 1.
Source of
Inspiration
French,
19th century

Figure 2.
Adaptation

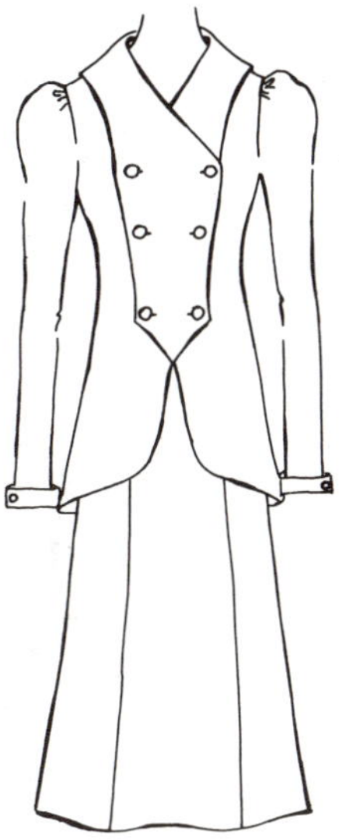

Figure 3.
Adaptation

Source material need not be limited to costumes. The shape of an object (right side up or even upside down), or a detail or trimming can also inspire fresh ideas.

CONTEMPORARY SOURCES

Contemporary sources of inspiration are restricted only to what the eye can see. Just as the textile designer often uses forms and colors from nature as a starting point for original prints, so may you, the clothes designer, look to your environment for endless subject matter. Nature, art, architecture, furniture, mechanical objects, space technology, posters, billboards, manhole covers, folk costumes, etc.—in short, everything around you is available for adaptation by the sharp eye and fertile mind.

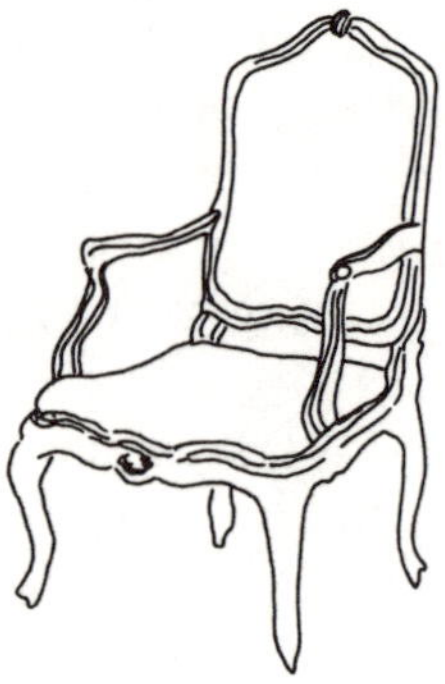

Figure 4.
Source of Inspiration

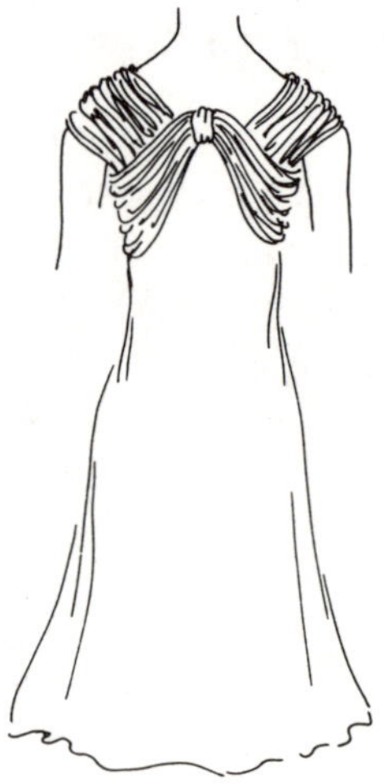

Figure 5.
Adaptation

Figure 6.
Source of Inspiration

Figure 7.
Adaptation

LESSON FOUR

trimming and fabric

TRIMMING

Trimming, because of its tremendous variety, has always provided a very rich source of inspiration for the designer. The photographs on the following pages demonstrate only a limited sample of is available.

Frogs: Used for closings, often found on mandarin-styled garments.

Ribbon

Appliqué: Pieces of trimming that are sewn on or applied to a costume.

Lace

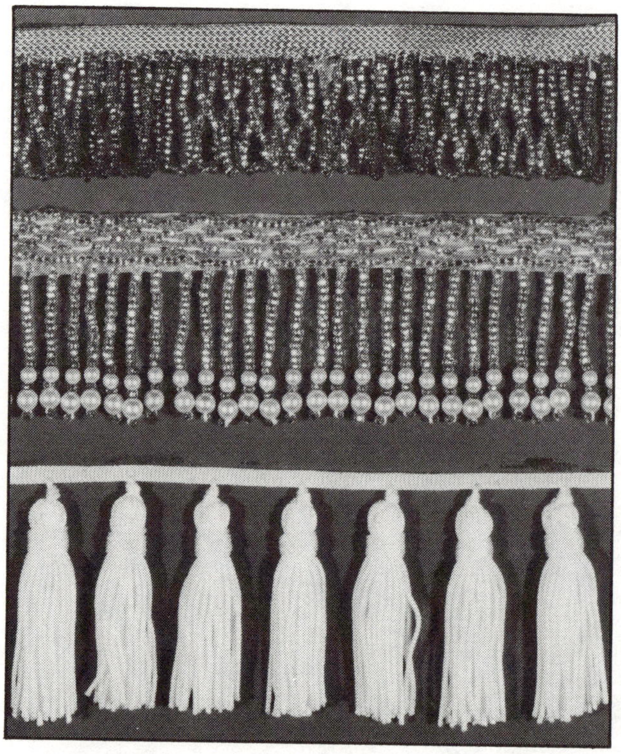

Fringe

Braid

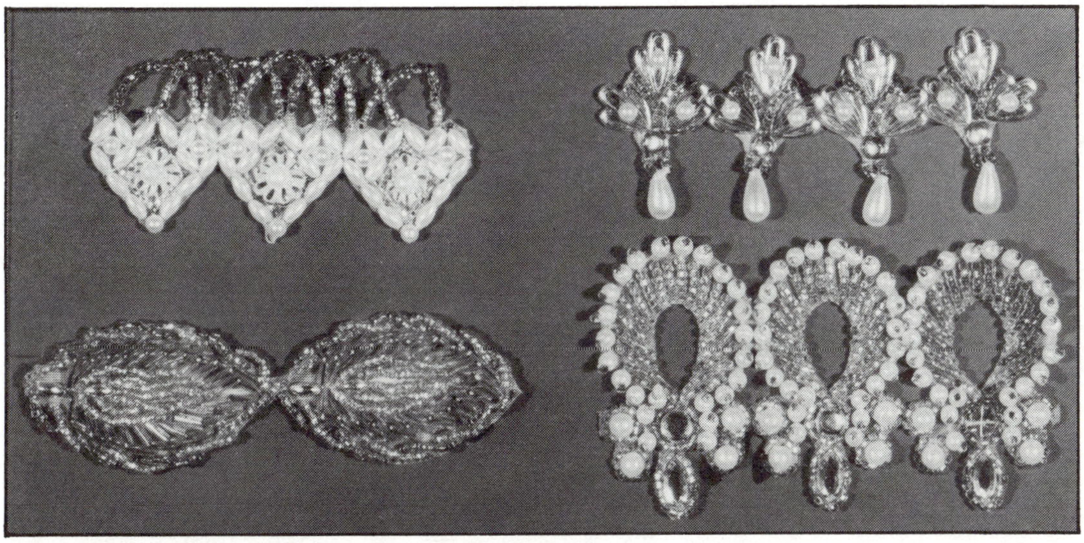

Beaded Appliqué

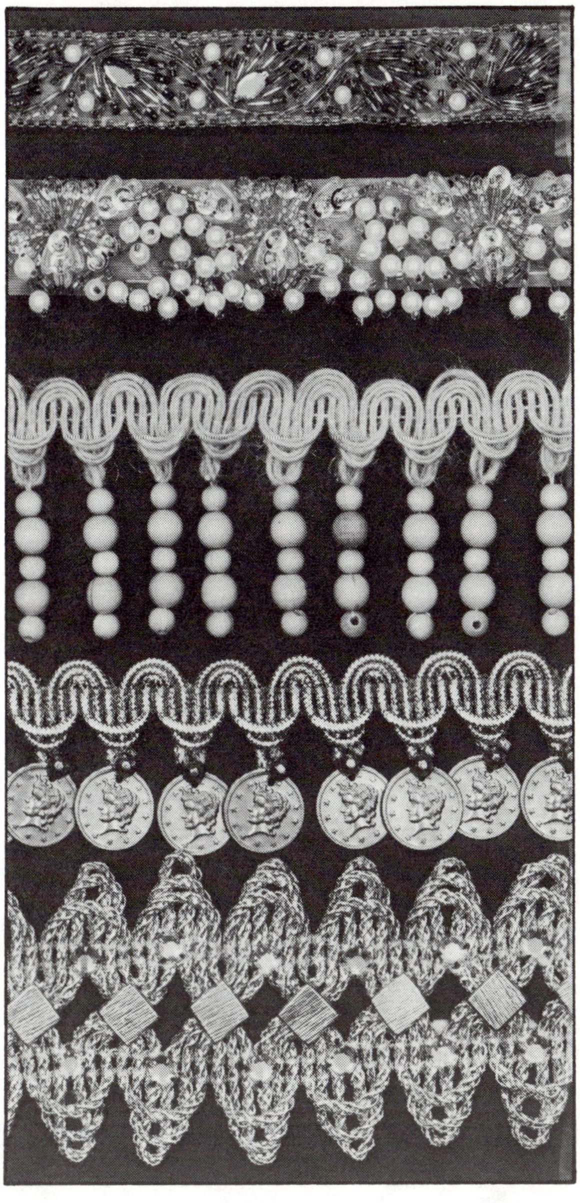

Novelty Trimmings:
Rhinestones, Beads, Coins,
Metallic Insets.

In addition to the trimmings in the photographs, other popular trimmings include buttons, bows, French knots, feathers, embroidery, eyelet, piping, binding, banding, cording, rickrack, sequins, ruching, fagoting, and various types of seaming and stitching. Also frequently used as design motifs are smocking, tucking, and scalloping.

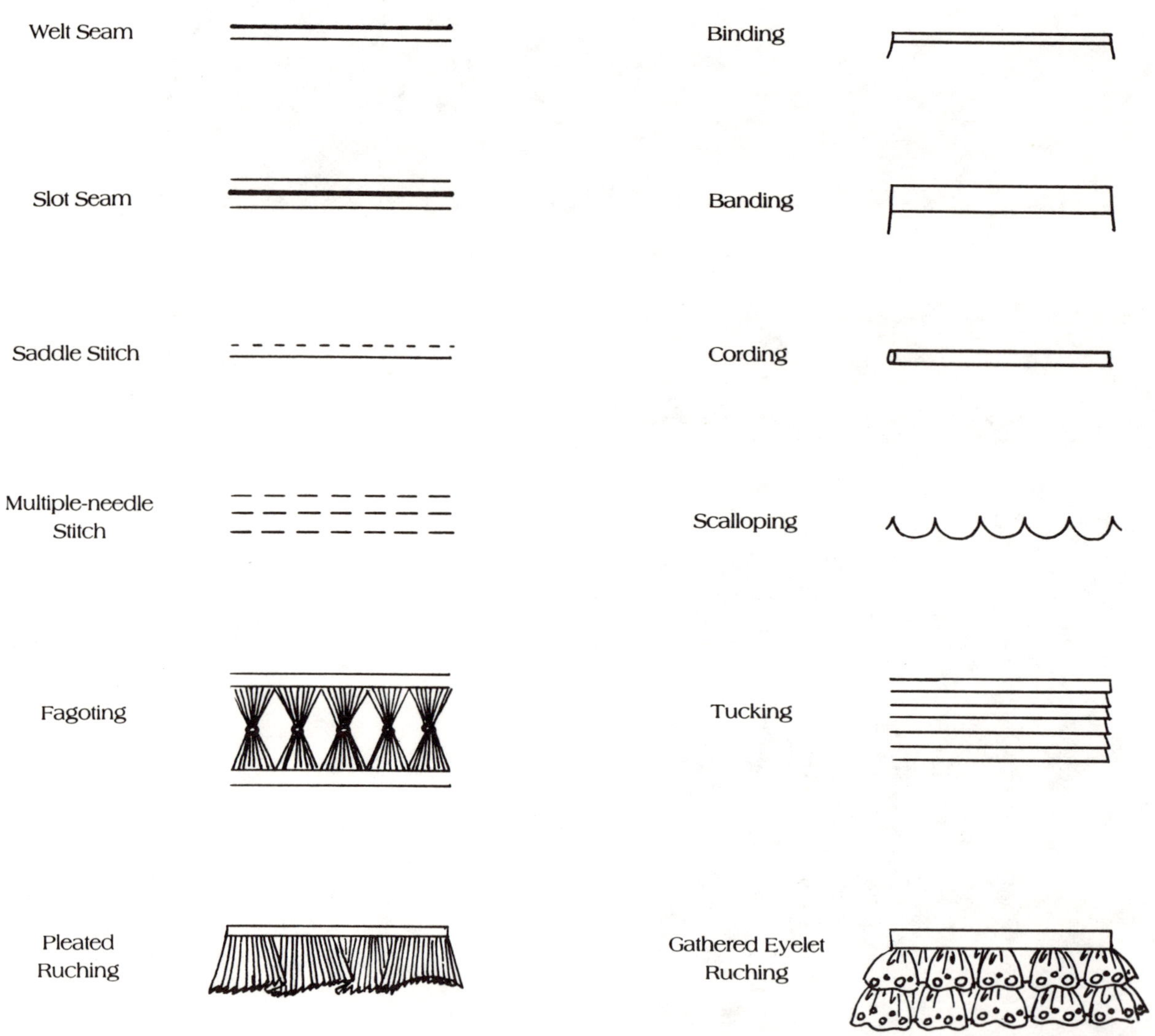

FABRIC

Fabric plays a significant role in the design of a costume. The weight, texture, and fiber content of any fabric dictates, to a great extent, the kind of garment which will be made from it. For example, a heavy, warm and nubby textured tweed wool would hardly be used to design a wedding dress or bathing suit. The fabric would more likely be used in the design of a winter suit or coat. A lightweight, quick-drying nylon stretch fabric immediately suggests designs for swimwear. A beautiful, transparent and filmy silk chiffon brings to mind the romantic and floating image of a lovely evening gown or elegant cocktail dress.

Fabric itself suggests to the creative designer the very best use to which that fabric can be put. That is how fabrics influence design.

UNIT 4
the front-view fashion figure

LESSON FIVE

developing the front-view croqui

The mastery of fashion sketching requires much time and effort. Students in special art schools might attend classes for as long as two years while developing this skill. There they often work from live models, learning how to draw the body in different fashion poses, and learning also various painting and other professional techniques.

But for the novice designer, an approach to sketching is required which does not take years to master—one that enables the beginner to quickly and simply illustrate original ideas. Such an approach makes use of the *croqui*, or undressed fashion figure. On the next few pages are examples of these which may be used for most of your early designing. But in order to develop your own croquis, and to understand the body's movement beneath its robes, knowing how to undress a figure is essential.

The general procedure is quite simple. A fashion figure is cut out of a pattern book or newspaper and placed on a drawing board with tracing paper over it. Both are secured with push pins or masking tape. Then it is undressed—that is, the body is redrawn without its garments, and special lines placed upon it. These lines correspond to those found on a dressmaker's model form. For the dressmaker they indicate placement of seams and darts; but for you they serve as drawing guides. The undressed figure on tracing paper is then mounted (pasted on a white background) so that it may be seen clearly, and is ready for use. When designing is about to begin, a blank sheet of tracing paper is placed over the croqui, and original ideas are worked around the croqui on the overlaying sheet of tracing paper.

These are "rough" sketches. A more polished technique of illustrating with color requires the use of vellum, and is dealt with in Unit 9.

UNDRESSING THE FRONT-VIEW FIGURE (Developing the Croqui)

1. A front-view figure faces you squarely. Both sides of the body are of approximately equal size. If one side is more prominent than the other, or if the figure is turned to one side, it is no longer a front-view figure.
2. Cut a front-view figure out of a pattern book or newspaper.
3. Place this clipping on your drawing board, with a sheet of tracing paper over it and secure with push pins or masking tape. Make sure the figure is standing up straight, and not tilting over.
4. Trace the parts of the body that are not covered by clothing, such as the face, neck, arms, hands, legs, etc.
5. Connect the neck to the outside edge of arms, and bring the inside edge of each arm up as high as the armpits—which are always slightly higher than the fullest part of the bust.
6. Analyze the figure. Does it have a high hip and low shoulder? This will influence the horizontal (those which go across) lines.

7. Draw all the horizontal lines in the following order:
   SHOULDERLINE From the tip of one shoulder to the other.
   BUSTLINE Through the apex (fullest part of bust); parallel to shoulderline.
   WAISTLINE Use inside of elbow as guide. If arms are raised, curve waistline down from inside of elbows.
   HEMLINE Follow hemline of garment.
   HIPLINE Approximately where legs start, parallel to hemline.

8. Draw all the vertical lines (those which go up and down).

   THE SIDES OF THE BODY In at the waist and out below, making a gentle curve.
   THE CENTER LINE This line divides the body approximately in half, and goes from the center of the shoulderline down to the hipline, but then branches out to become the inside of the thighs. Buttons, bows, belts, seams, etc., may be used as guides for finding the center line.
   THE SHOULDER-DART LINES On the shoulderline, divide the distance between the center of the neck and the edge of the shoulder in half. From there, draw lines down to the bustline parallel to the center line. Above the shoulderline, these lines curve out.

The Front-View Fashion Figure

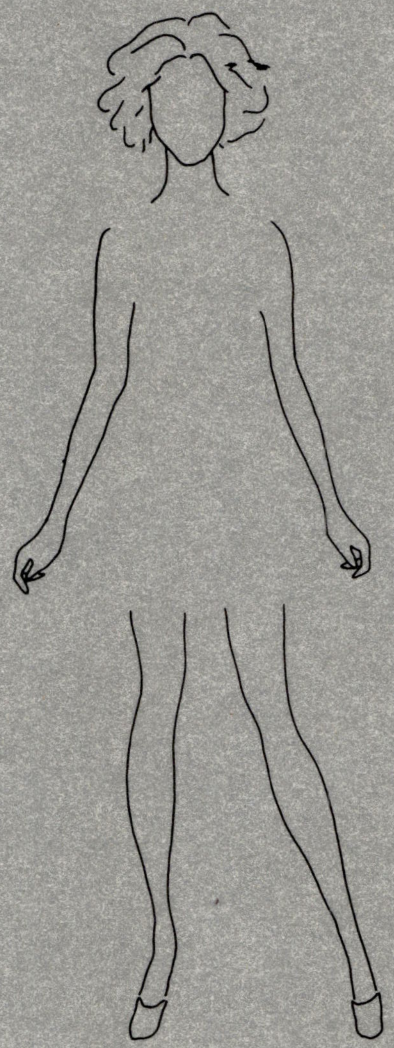

Figure 1.
Trace parts of body not covered by clothing.

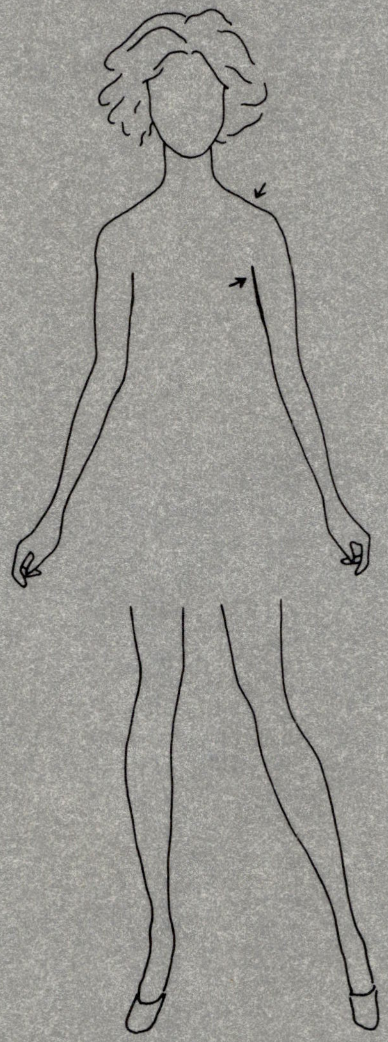

Figure 2.
Connect neck to outside edge of arms. Draw inside of arm higher than bustline.

Figure 3.
Draw all horizontal lines.

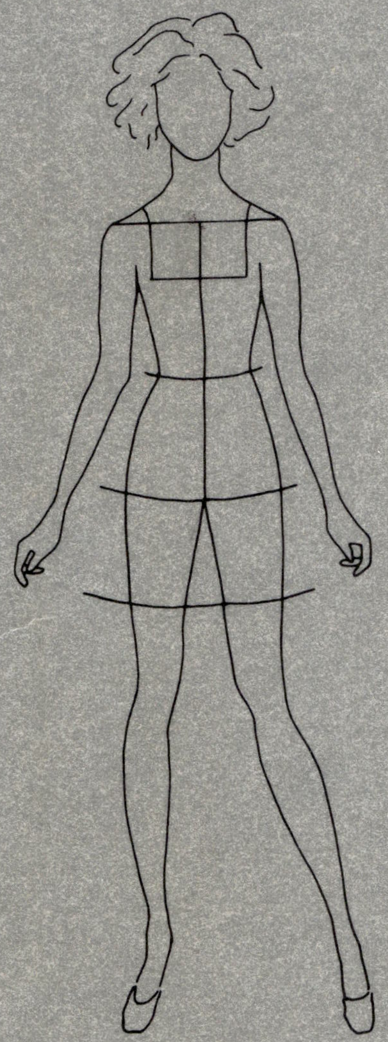

Figure 4.
Draw all vertical lines.

The Front-View Fashion Figure

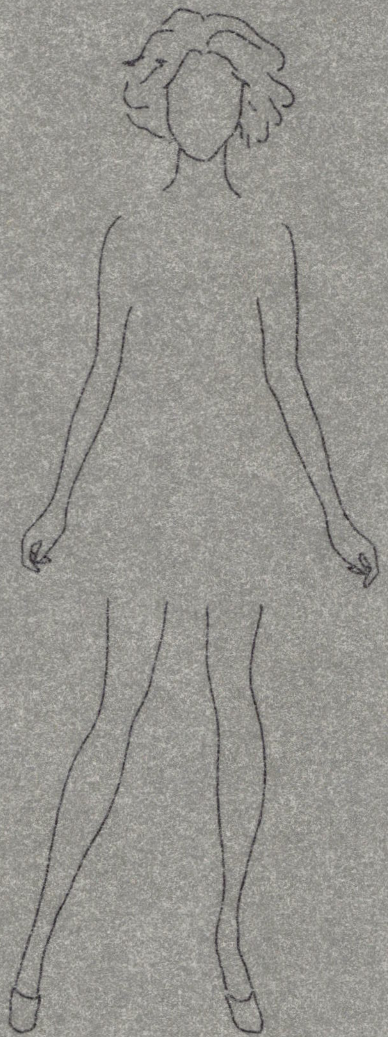

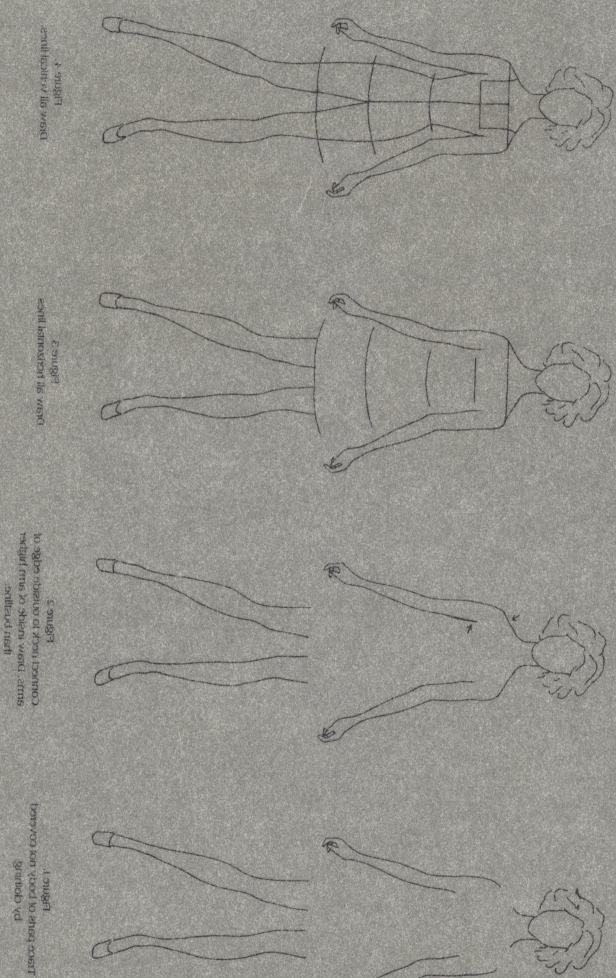

Figure 1.
Trace parts of body not covered by clothing.

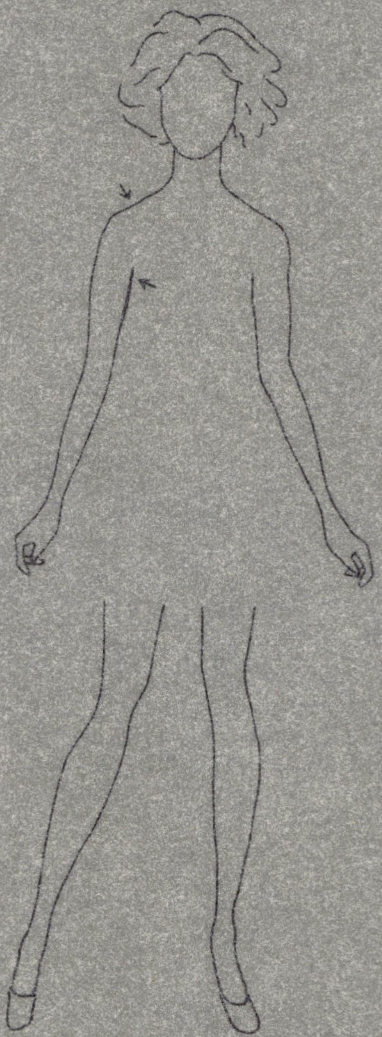

Figure 2.
Connect neck to outside edge of arms. Draw inside of arm higher than bustline.

Figure 3.
Draw all horizontal lines.

Figure 4.
Draw all vertical lines.

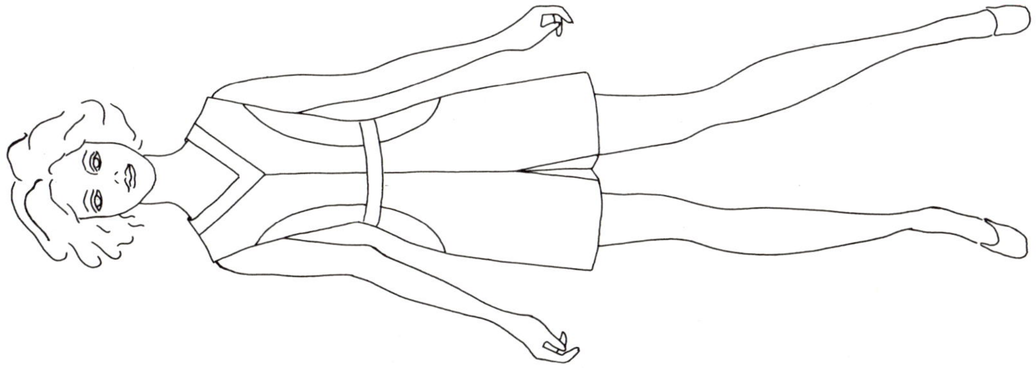

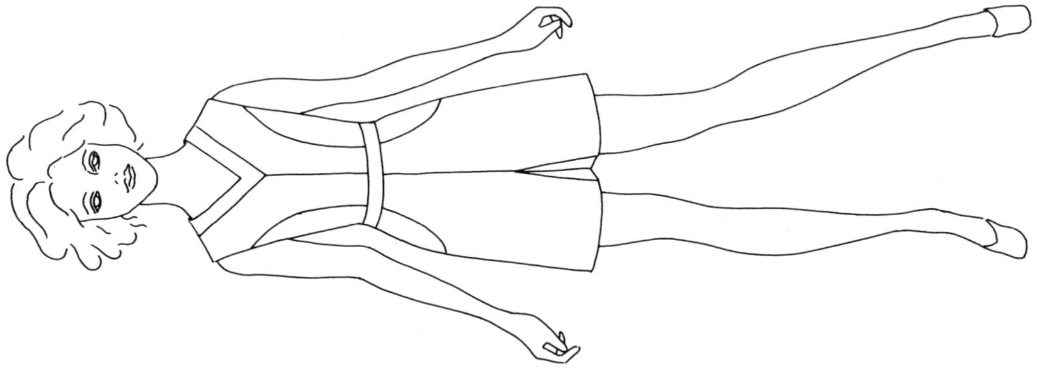

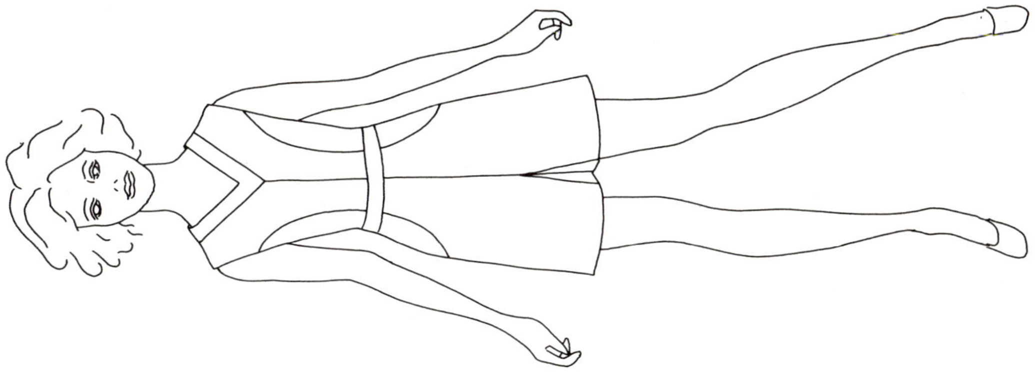

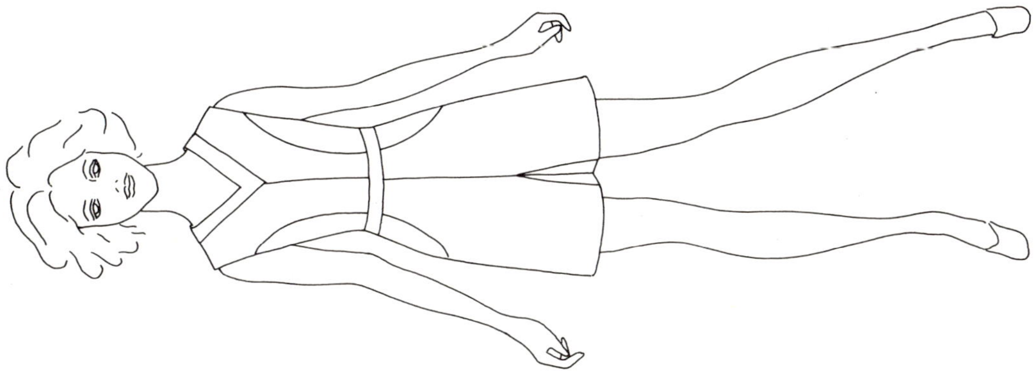

LESSON SIX

undressing the front-view figure

On the following pages are four front-view fashion figures. Each one is illustrated both dressed and undressed. Although the undressed figures (croquis) may be used for most of your designing purposes, every attempt should be made to learn how to develop the croqui.

By completing Exercises 1, 2, 3, and 4 according to instructions, you will greatly improve your drawing ability, knowledge of anatomy, and ability to undress any front-view fashion figure.

IMPORTANT Do not discard any dressed or undressed figures, since they will be called for again in future lessons.

Figure 5. Undressed

Figure 6. Dressed

EXERCISE 1

You may correct your undressed figure by placing it over this one and checking for mistakes.

Place a sheet of tracing paper over this figure and secure with masking tape. Undress according to instructions on pages 23 and 24.

Figure 7. Dressed

Figure 8. Undressed

EXERCISE 2

Place a sheet of tracing paper over this figure and secure with masking tape. Undress according to instructions on pages 23 and 24.

You may correct your undressed figure by placing it over this one and checking for mistakes.

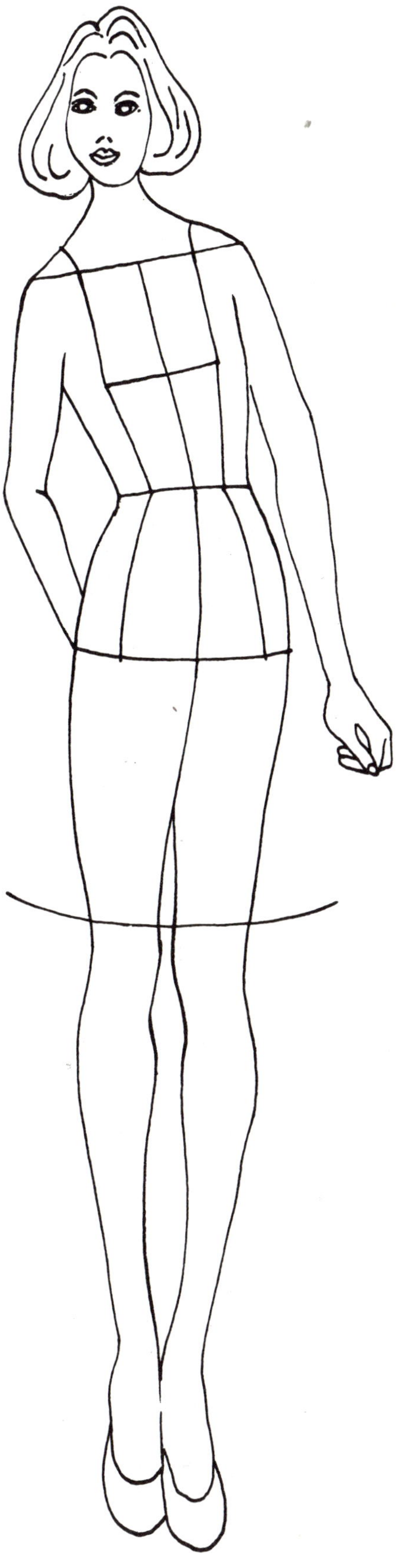

Figure 9. Undressed

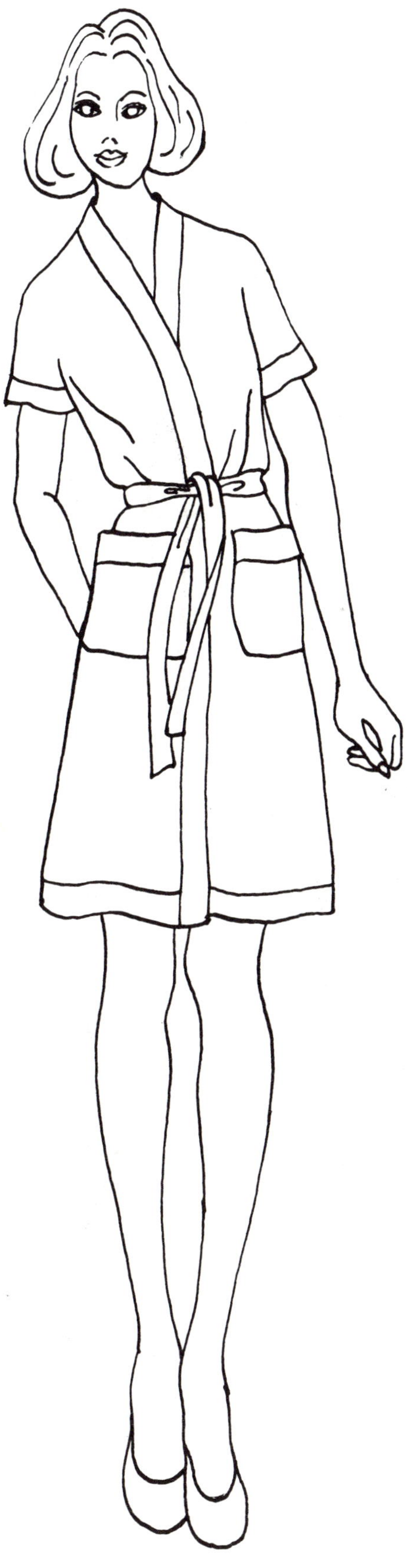

Figure 10. Dressed

EXERCISE 3

You may correct your undressed figure by placing it over this one and checking for mistakes.

Place a sheet of tracing paper over this figure and secure with masking tape. Undress according to instructions on pages 23 and 24.

Figure 11. Dressed

Figure 12. Undressed

EXERCISE 4

Place a sheet of tracing paper over this figure and secure with masking tape. Undress according to instructions on pages 23 and 24.

You may correct your undressed figure by placing it over this one and checking for mistakes.

UNIT 5 the basic pattern or "sloper"

LESSON SEVEN

basic darts and their variations

The basic fitted pattern, from which all other patterns are made, is known as a *sloper*. Illustrated here are the basic slopers for the front and back fitted tops and skirts. The basic darts for these slopers serve the purpose of removing excess fabric fullness, which enables a garment to fit smoothly over the shape of the body beneath it.

Basic Slopers

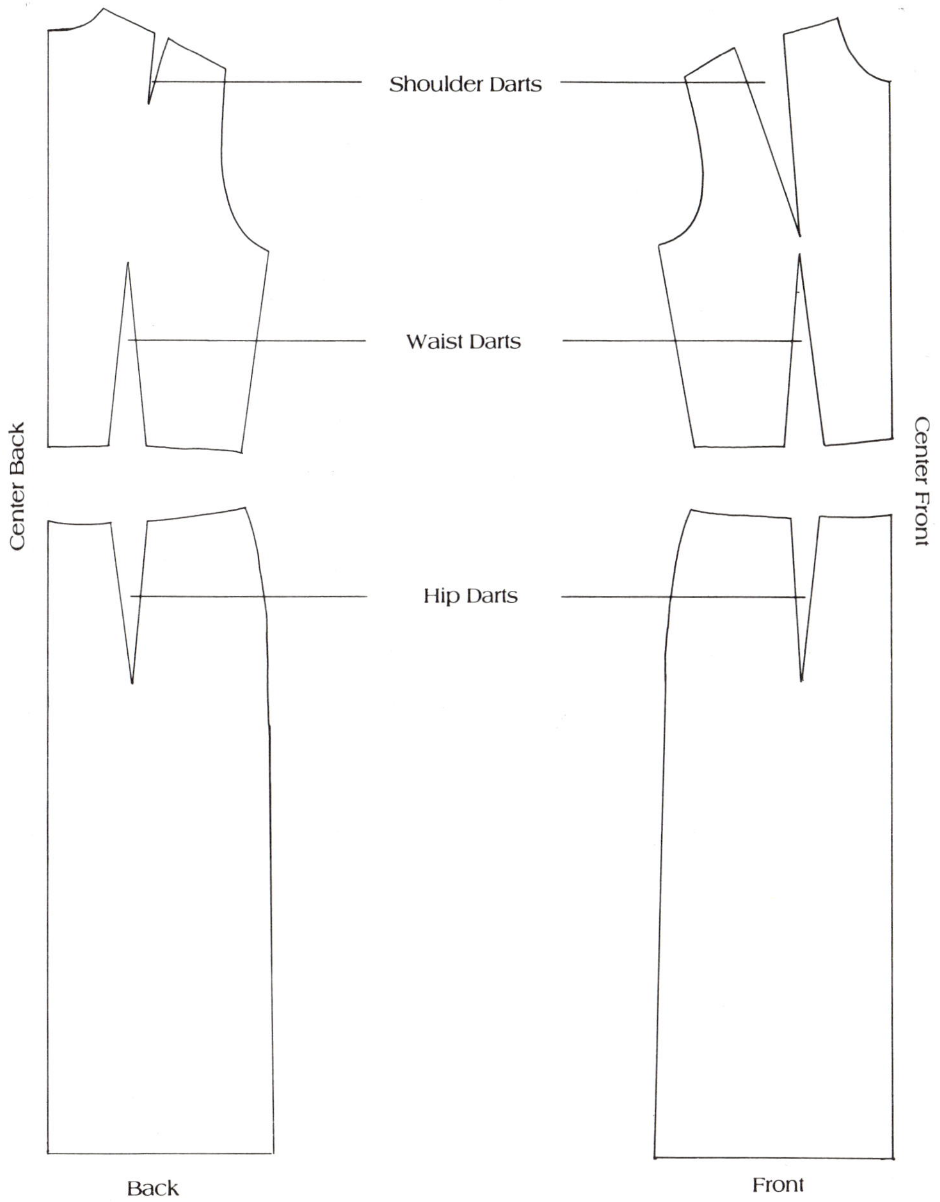

The patternmaker designs original patterns by drafting changes in the basic slopers. For example, in the patterns illustrated below, the shoulder dart of the basic sloper (page 35), is replaced by a variety of other bust darts.

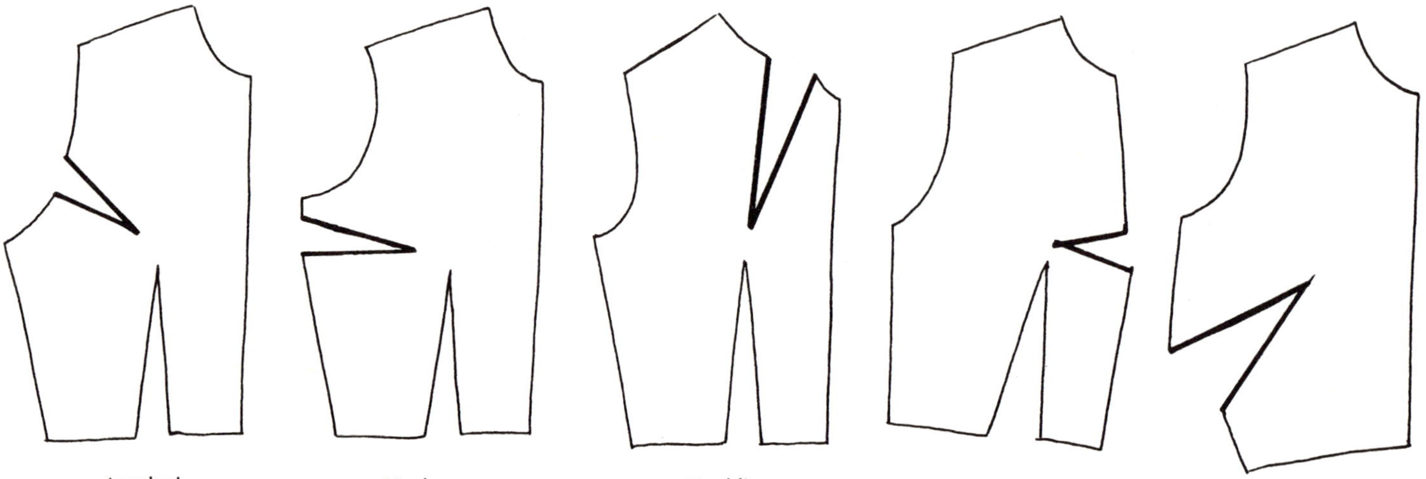

Armhole Dart | Underarm Dart | Neckline Dart | Center Front Dart | French Dart

BUST DART VARIATIONS OF THE FRONT SLOPER

Each bust dart (heavy outlines) serves the same purpose as the shoulder dart. That is, they all remove excess fabric fullness caused by the contour of the bust. The French dart, however, removes the bust and waist fullness, thereby substituting for both darts of the basic top front sloper.

The drawings below show how the darts would look when sewn together as part of a completed garment.

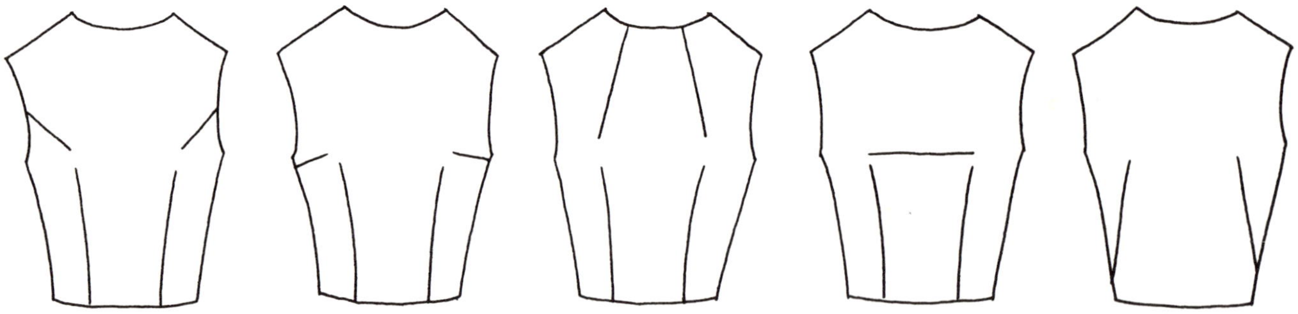

Armhole Darts | Underarm Darts | Neckline Darts | Center Front Darts | French Darts

LESSON EIGHT

connecting darts to create seams

As you have seen in the previous lesson, darts are used to fit a garment to the body. Seams are used for exactly the same reason, but in addition may be used for styling. They play an important part not only in the construction, but also in the design of a costume.

How do we get a seam? Where does it come from? One way to get a seam is to connect darts. For example: Figure 1 is a fitted top with shoulder and waist darts. Figure 2 is a fitted top with shoulder and waist darts connected to create seams.

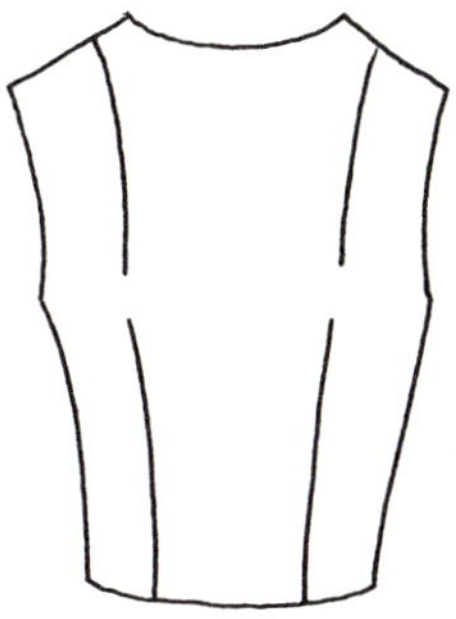

Figure 1. Fitted top with shoulder and waist darts.

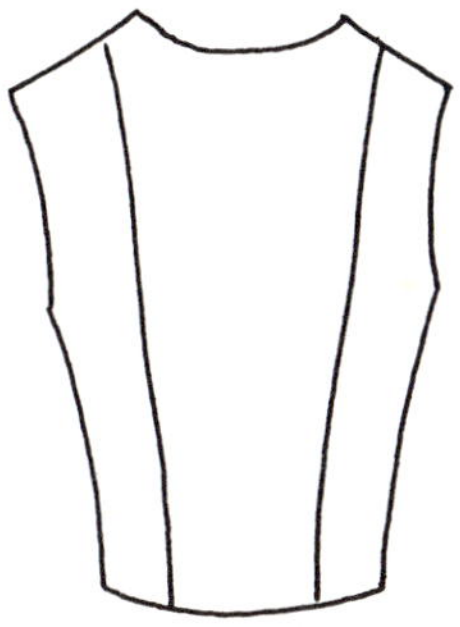

Figure 2. Fitted top with shoulder and waist darts connected to create seams.

EXERCISE 1

On the drawings below, connect the bust darts to the waist darts to create seams.

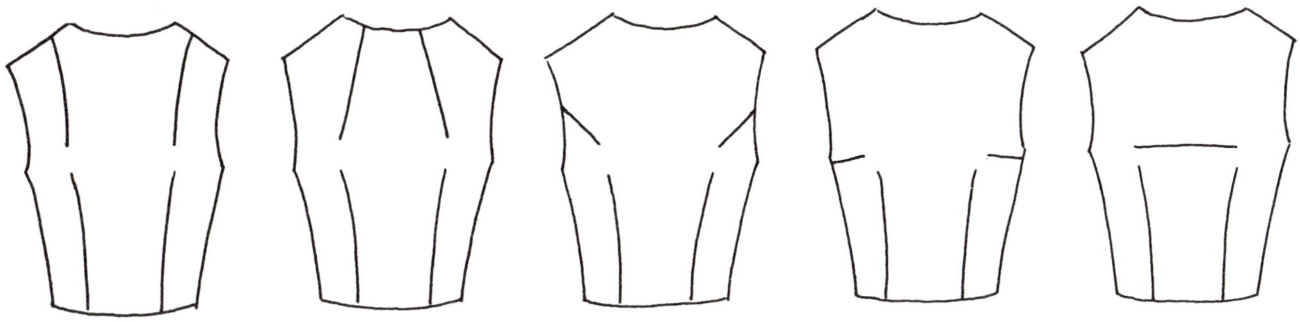

Figure 3

In addition to the seams you have just created, many unusual and interesting seamlines can be designed simply by connecting darts in different combinations. For example, the drawings below illustrate seams that were designed by connecting various bust and waist darts.

Figure 4

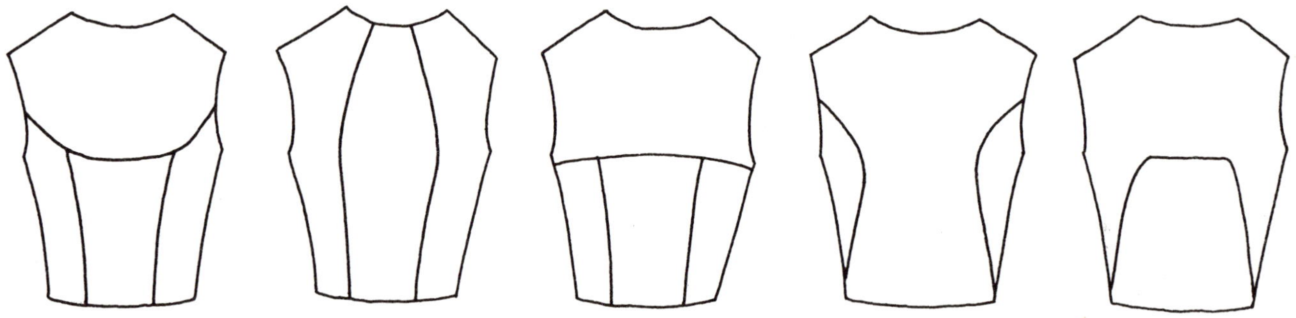

A B C D E

EXERCISE 2

In the spaces provided below, label the darts which make up the seams in each drawing of Figure 4. (See page 36 for names of darts.)

A. ______________, ______________, and ______________ darts.

B. ______________ and ______________ darts.

C. ______________, ______________, and ______________ darts.

D. ______________ and ______________ darts.

E. ______________ and ______________ darts.

EXERCISE 3

Place a sheet of tracing paper over the croquis provided here. Design at least ten fitted tops with seams. Label each design with the names of the darts you used to create your original seamlines. *Before starting,* study the next page carefully.

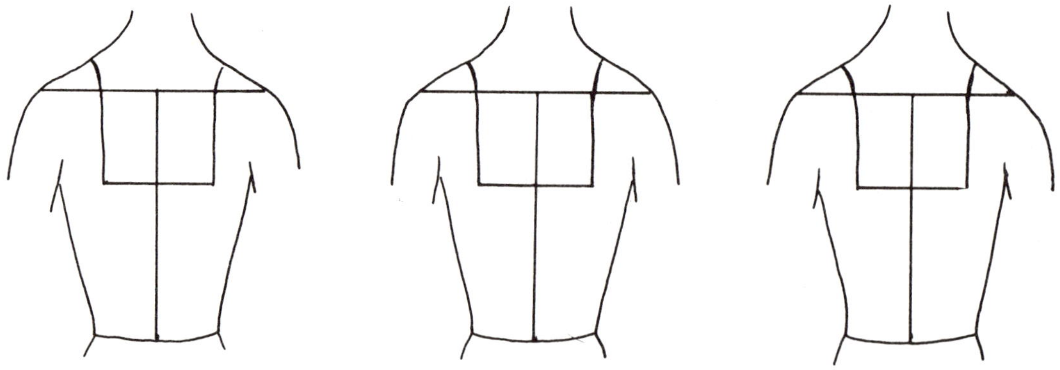

POINTS TO REMEMBER—ERRORS TO AVOID

1. Both bust darts and waist darts are necessary to fit a top. Therefore, a French dart or a waist dart is required in every one of your designs.
   NOTE Actually, it is possible to fit a garment with one dart (other than the French dart), but is not often done. For the purpose of this lesson, let us adhere to the bust and waist dart requirement.

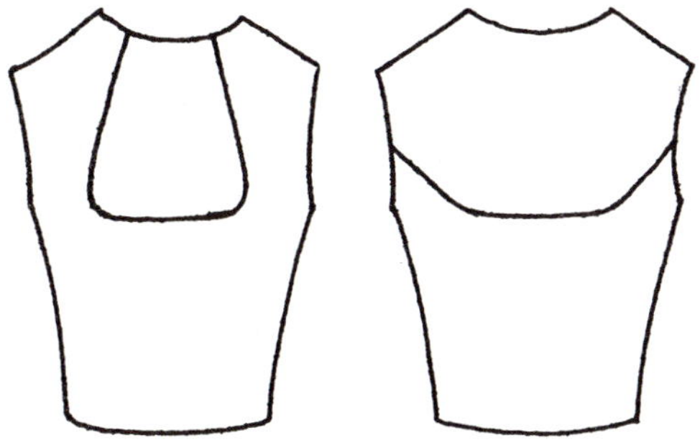

Figure 5. Incorrect
How can these fit the waist without darts?

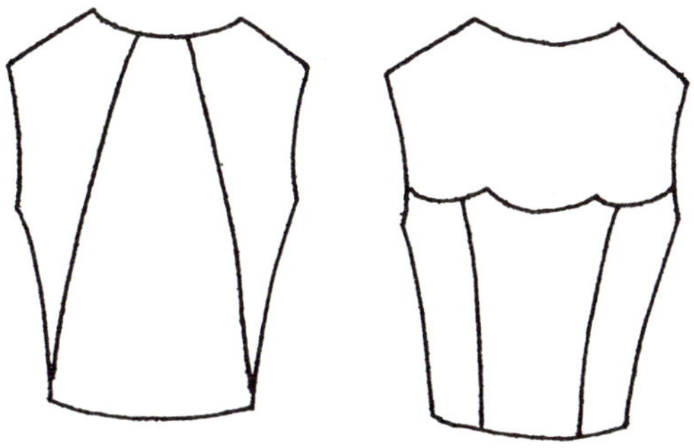

Figure 6. Correct
Waist or French darts are included.

2. At least one seam should intersect (or cross) the apex of the bust. If not, then two other methods of dealing with the excess fabric fullness caused by the contour of the bust may be used. First, a dart may extend from a seam toward the apex of the bust; and second, shirring can replace this dart. A third alternative, the "shrinking in" of excess fabric, is an advanced design technique and therefore not dealt with here.

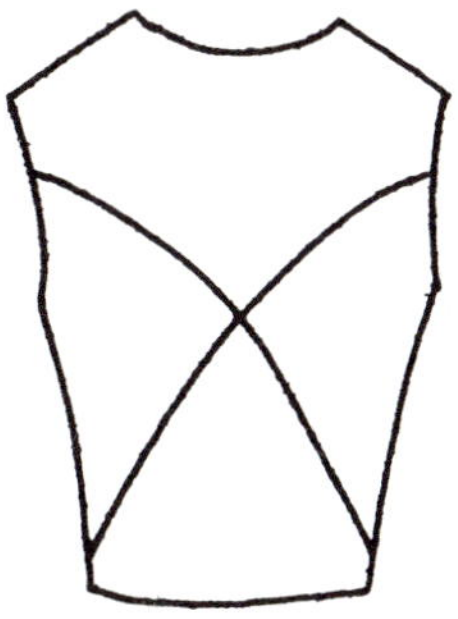

Figure 7. Incorrect
Apex of bust has no seam intersecting it.

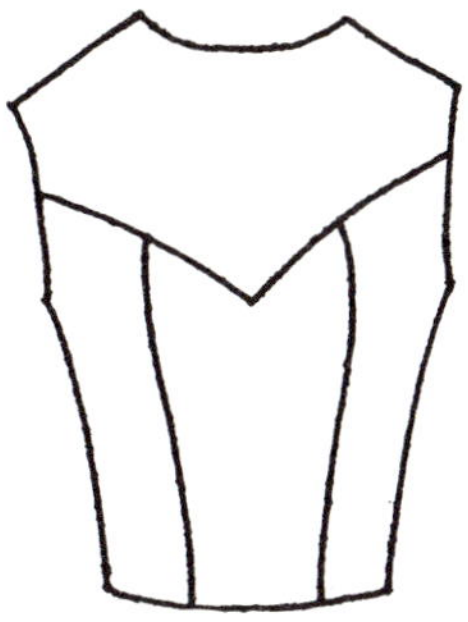

Figure 8. Correct
Apex of bust has a seam intersecting it.

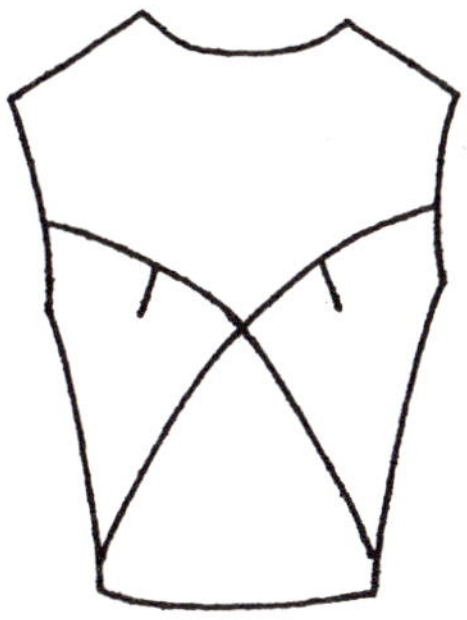

Figure 9. Correct
Dart extends from seam to apex of bust.

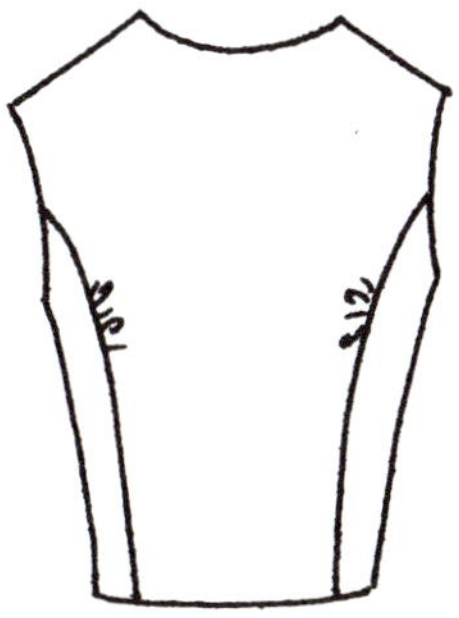

Figure 10. Correct
Shirring extending from seam replaces dart.

REFERENCES FOR FURTHER READING

For those of you interested in exploring patternmaking, an excellent and comprehensive book is *Designing Apparel through the Flat Pattern,* by Kopp, Rolfo, Zelin, and Gross, published by Fairchild Publications.

UNIT 6 basic silhouettes

LESSON NINE

basic silhouettes

Fitted Waist

Fitted Princess

Semi-fitted Princess

A-line

Shift

In fashion, a silhouette refers to the shape of a costume. Shown here are the most popular silhouettes of the past few decades.

Silhouettes rely upon the use of particular darts and seams for their characteristic shapes. The designer must know how each is constructed—which darts and seams may be used, and where to place them.

Chemise

Tent

Blouson

Sheath

Empire

FITTED WAIST

The fitted waist refers to any dress that is snugly fitted on top, either by darts or seams, and sewn to the skirt (skirt shape is optional) at the waistline.

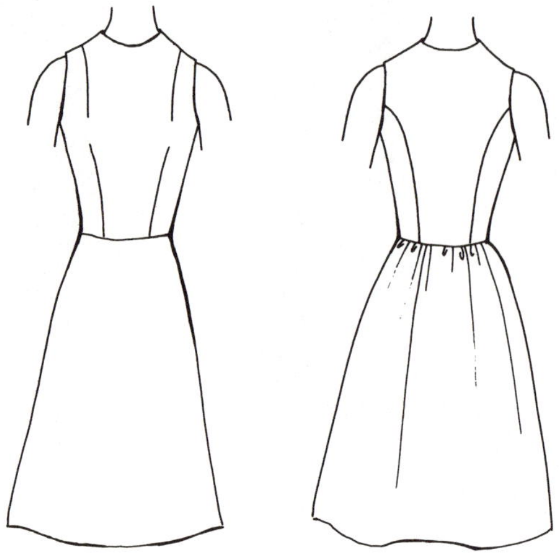

Fitted Waist

FITTED PRINCESS

The fitted princess neatly hugs the body, is nipped in at the waist, and flares out below the waist. It is shaped by the traditional princess seams. If extra skirt fullness is desired, additional seams (such as center front and back) may be added.

Fitted Princess

SEMI-FITTED PRINCESS

The semi-fitted princess is looser at the waist than the princess, and the skirt is less flared. It derives its shape from a variety of interesting seam combinations.

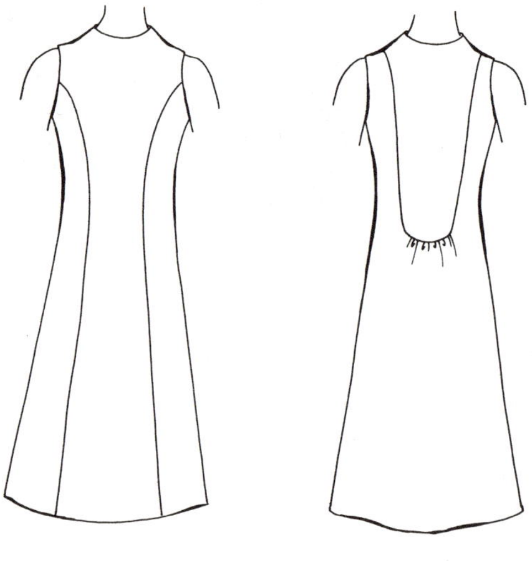

Semi-fitted Princess

A-LINE

This silhouette strongly resembles the semi-fitted princess silhouette. It differs primarily in construction, for only a French dart is required to shape the A-line. The French dart is sometimes combined with bust darts for design purposes.

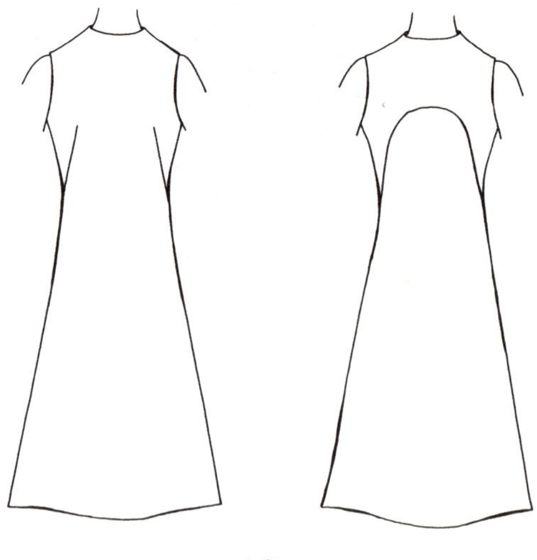

A-line

SHIFT

The shift has always been popular with designers of women's sizes, because its straight lines tend to hide the figure beneath it. Only a set of bust darts is required—either the basic shoulder dart, or any of its variations. (See page 36 for bust-dart variations.)

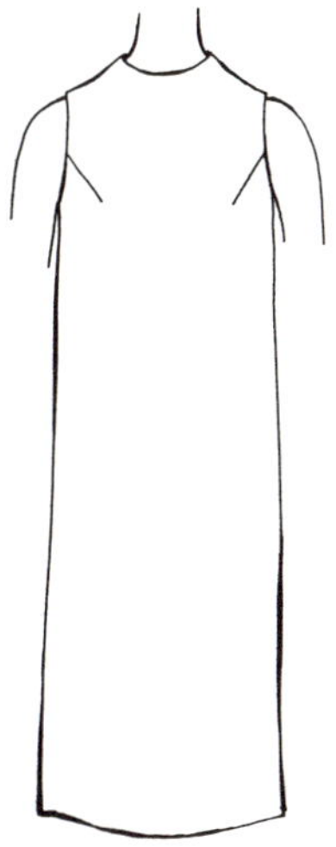

Shift

CHEMISE

The chemise, like the shift, is loose about the waist. Unlike the shift, it is often tighter at the hips, and the skirt is not necessarily straight—it may be gored, pegged, draped, etc.

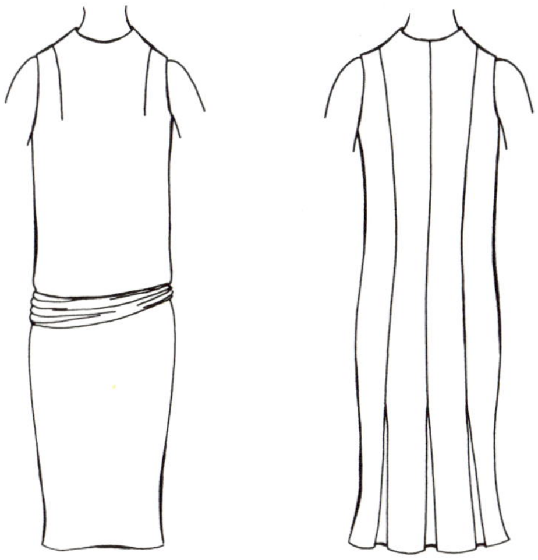

Chemise

TENT

The tent is most popular in maternity and extra-large sizes. It flares out from below the armhole, making an underarm dart impractical. Any other bust dart will do.

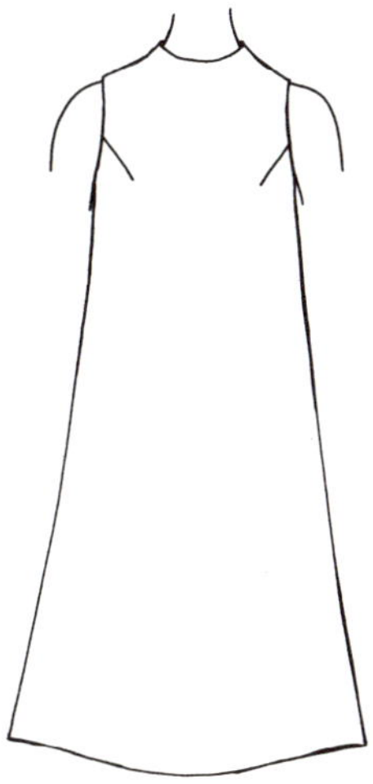

Tent

BLOUSON

The blouson refers to any dress whose top blouses over its skirt, either at the waistline or more often, below it. Any bust dart or skirt shape is appropriate.

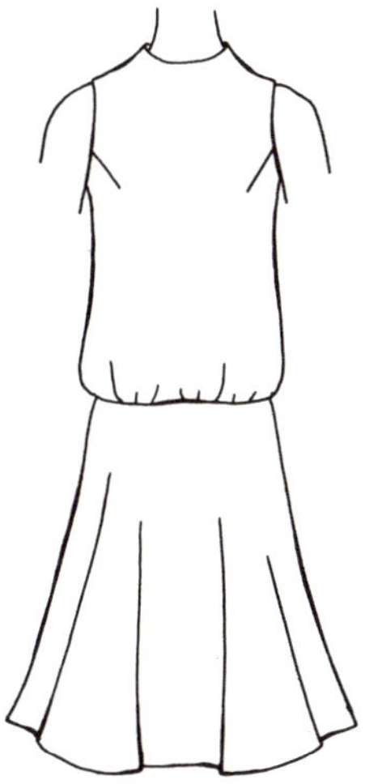

Blouson

SHEATH

The sheath is closely fitted, usually by darts, infrequently by seams, and has no waistline seam.

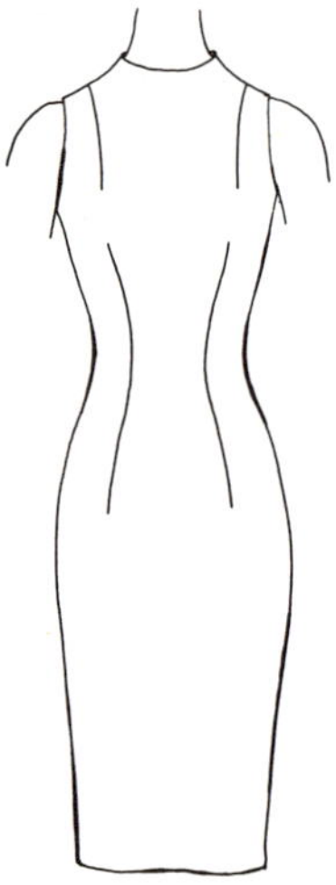

Sheath

EMPIRE

The empire has a seam below the bust. Appropriate darts are under the bust, but seams are often used to shape the top, while the shape of the skirt varies.

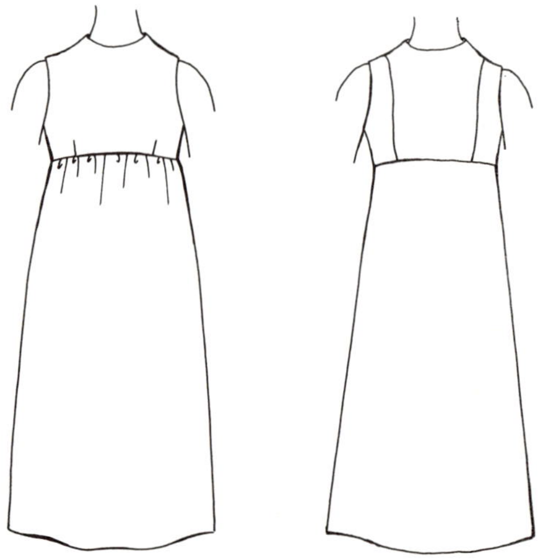

Empire

LESSON TEN

exercises

EXERCISE 1 DRAWING THE SILHOUETTES

Place a piece of tracing paper over a croqui from Unit 4. Draw each silhouette. Complete nine drawings, one for each silhouette.

NOTE When dressing the croqui, the garment is drawn outside the body just as when you undressed the figure, the body was drawn inside the garment.

EXERCISE 2 FILLING IN APPROPRIATE DARTS AND/OR SEAMS

On each of the nine silhouettes which you have just drawn, insert the proper darts and/or seams. Can you remember enough to do it on your own? If so, when you are finished, refer back to the text and correct your work. Label each silhouette.

UNIT 7 basic necklines

LESSON ELEVEN

BASIC NECKLINES

- High Neckline
- Round (or Jewel) Neckline
- Halter Neckline
- Boat Neckline
- Keyhole Neckline
- Cowl Neckline
- Scoop (or U-shape) Neckline
- Square Neckline
- Sweetheart Neckline
- V-shape Neckline
- Surplice Neckline

LESSON TWELVE

EXERCISE 1 DRAWING NECKLINES

EXERCISE 2 DRAWING NECKLINES ON THREE-QUARTER-VIEW FIGURES

LESSON ELEVEN

basic necklines

Basic necklines are generally either round, oval, scooped, square, or V-shaped. Countless variations are possible.

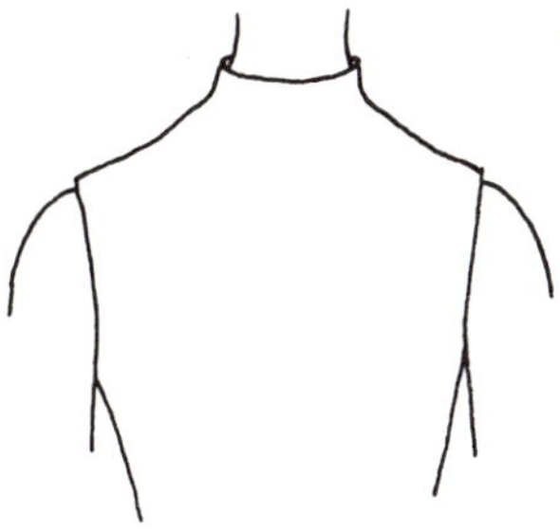

high
neckline

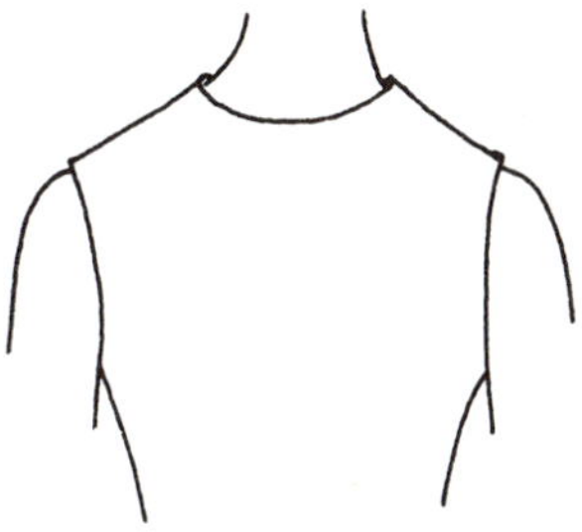

round (or jewel)
neckline

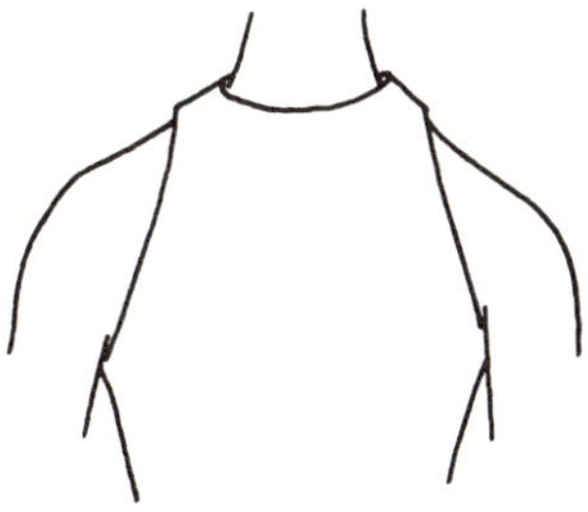

halter
neckline

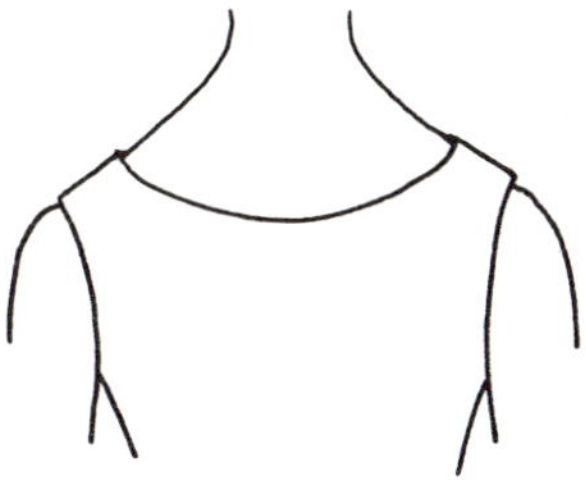

boat
neckline

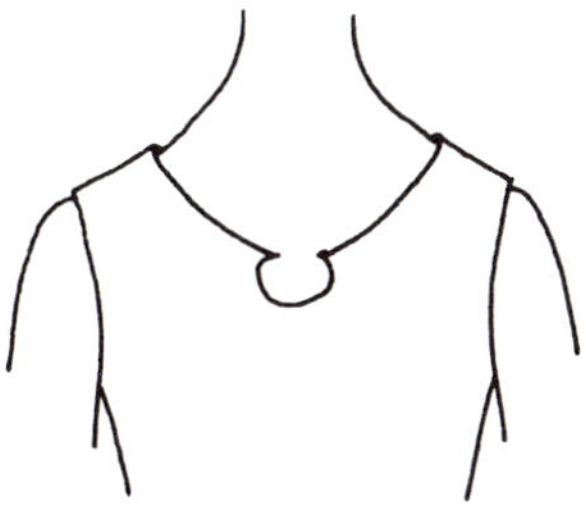

keyhole
neckline

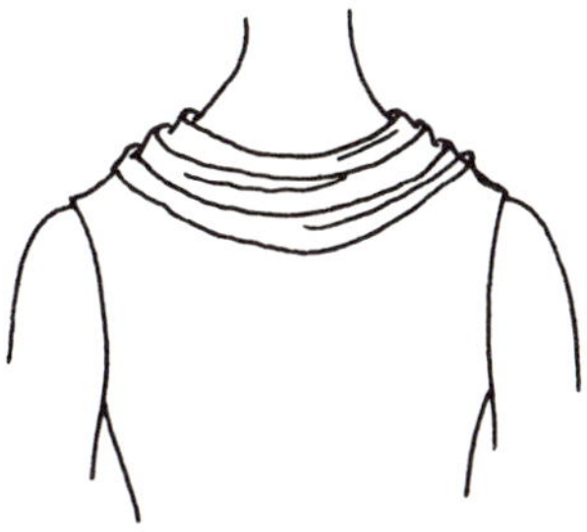

cowl
neckline

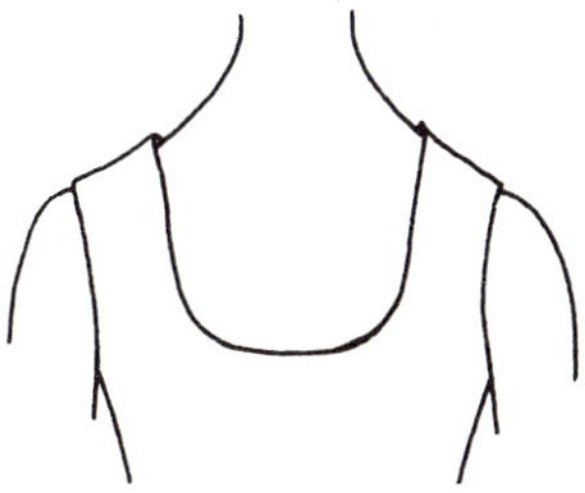

scoop (or U-shape)
neckline

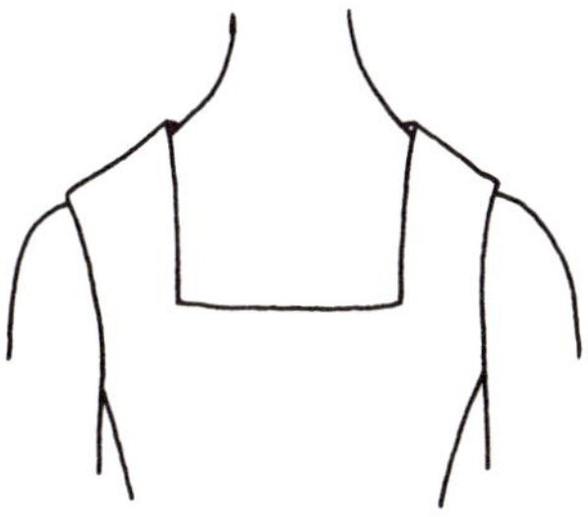

square
neckline

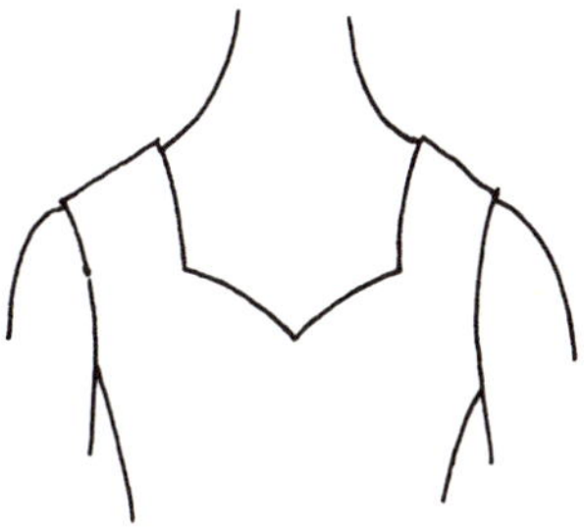

sweetheart
neckline

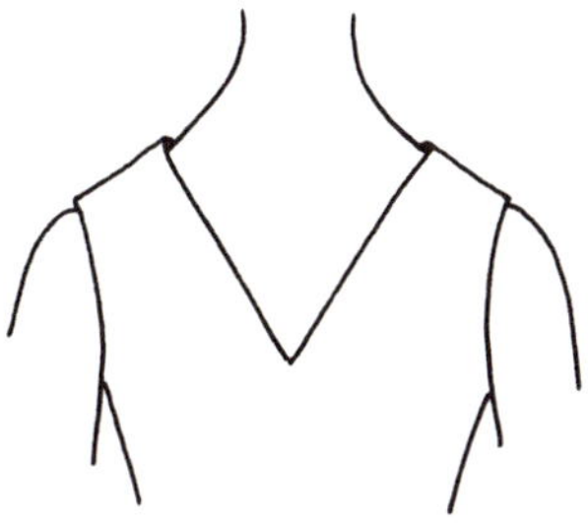

V-shape
neckline

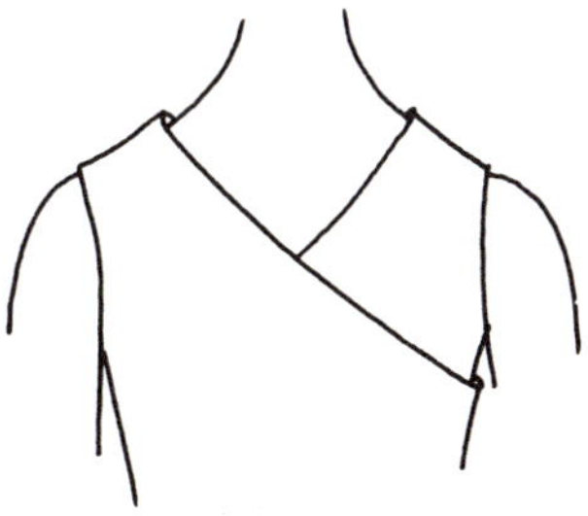

surplice
neckline

LESSON TWELVE

exercises

EXERCISE 1 DRAWING NECKLINES

Place a piece of tracing paper over Figure 1. Draw the following necklines: high, round, halter, boat, keyhole, cowl, scoop, square, sweetheart, V-neck, and surplice.

Check your work by matching each drawing with the correct ones on page 53.

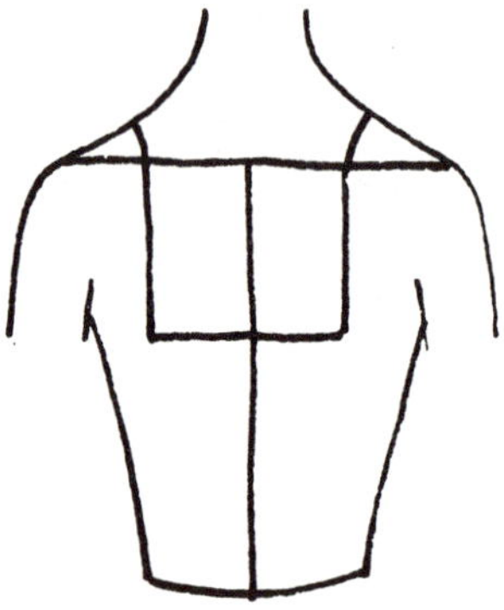

Figure 1

EXERCISE 2 DRAWING NECKLINES ON THREE-QUARTER-VIEW FIGURES

Illustrated below are some basic necklines on a body which is not front view but turned slightly to the side (three-quarter view).

Place a piece of tracing paper over Figure 2. Draw the basic necklines just as they are shown here. Study them carefully. Label each neckline.

NOTE The center line on a three-quarter-view figure is not in the middle.

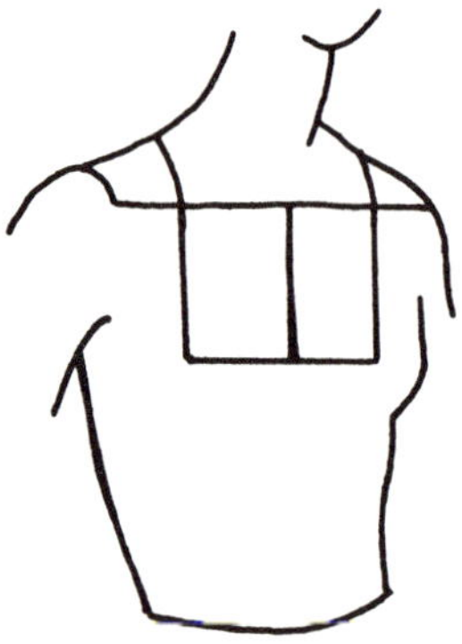

Figure 2

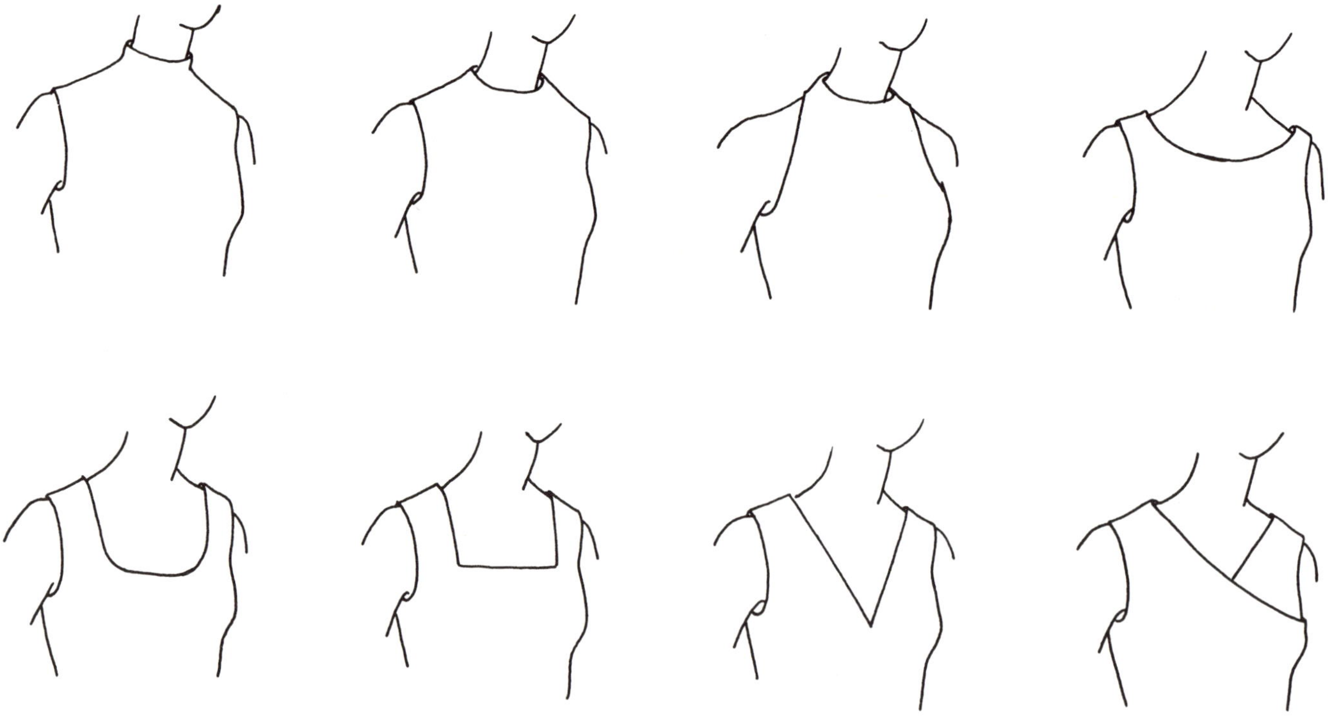

UNIT 8 designing with seams

LESSON THIRTEEN

darts into seams

In Unit 5, you connected the darts on a fitted top to create some interesting seams. The same approach may be applied to the design of an entire dress.

In order to achieve the silhouettes you see in Figures 1 and 2, either darts or seams are necessary. Both darts or seams remove excess fabric fullness, enabling the garment to fit smoothly at the bust, taper in at the waist, and out again at the hips.

Princess seams (Figure 2) are obtained by combining the basic bust, waist, and hip darts shown in Figure 1. The advantage of seams over darts is that they offer greater styling flexibility. For example, if other bust darts are combined with waist and hip darts, then different effects are achieved.

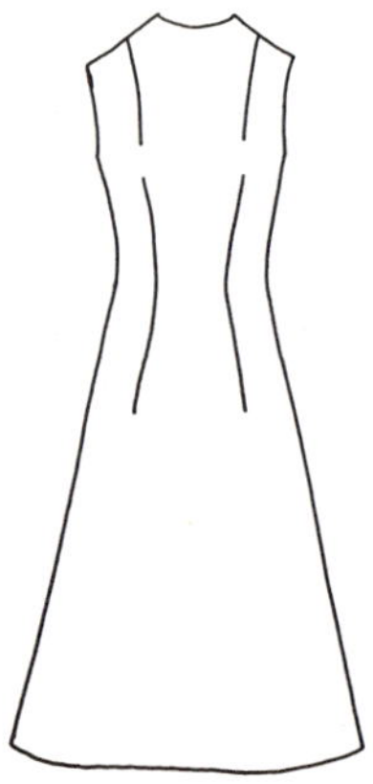

Figure 1. Bust, Waist, and Hip Darts

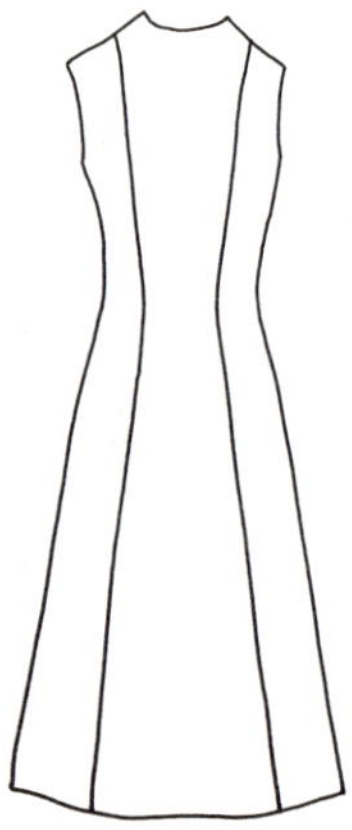

Figure 2 Princess Seams

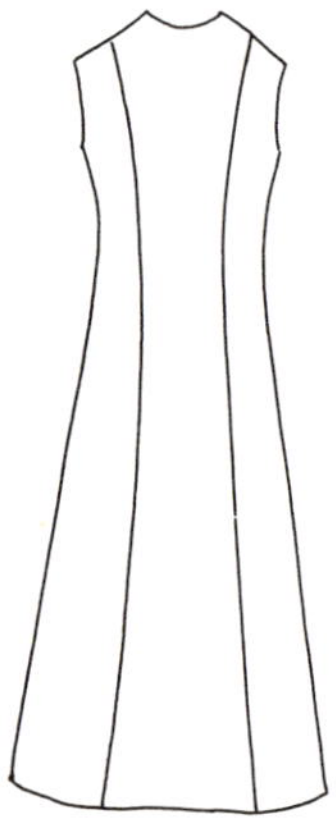

A

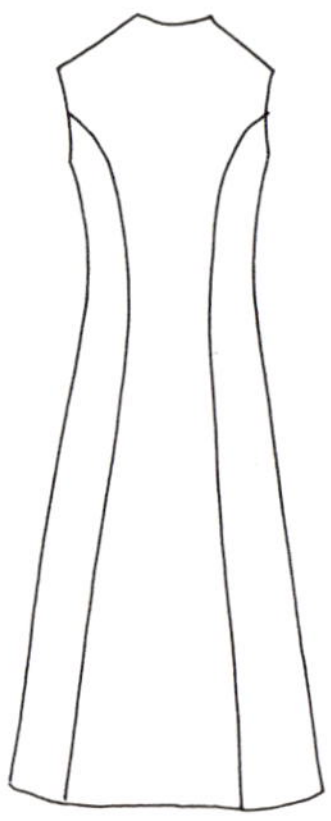

B

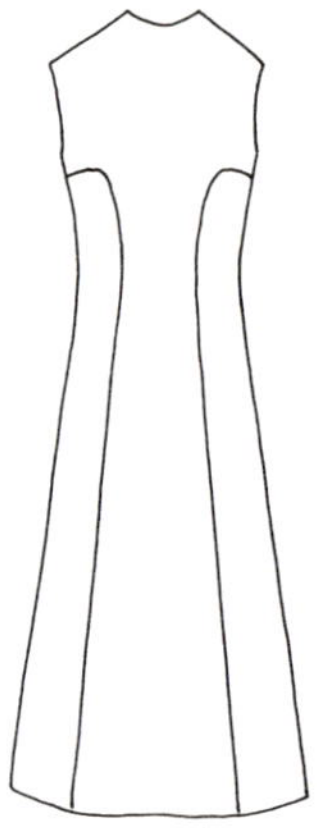

C

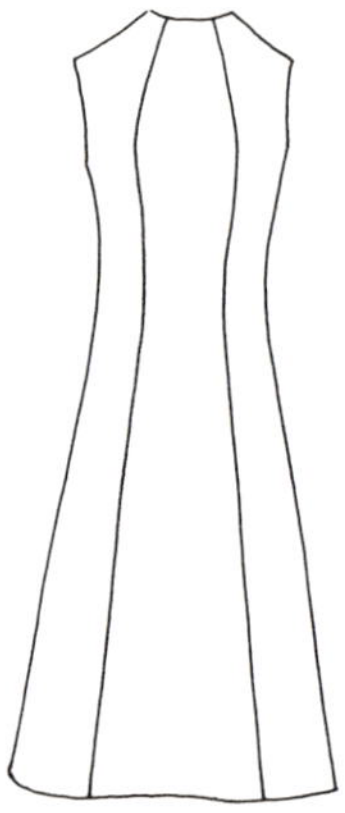

D

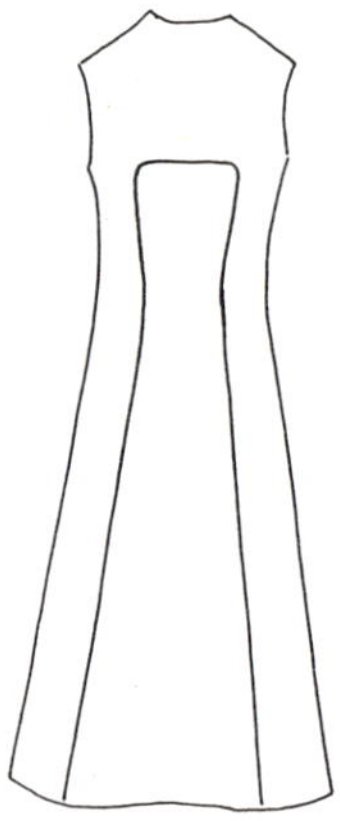

E

EXERCISE 1

Name the bust darts that went into each of the princess dresses above.

A. ________________________________

B. ________________________________

C. ________________________________

D. ________________________________

E. ________________________________

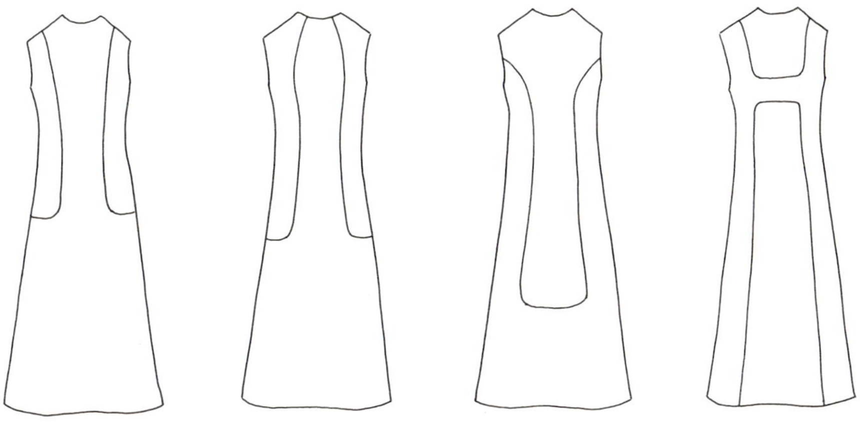

Additional changes in the basic dart connections provide an even broader scope of design possibilities.

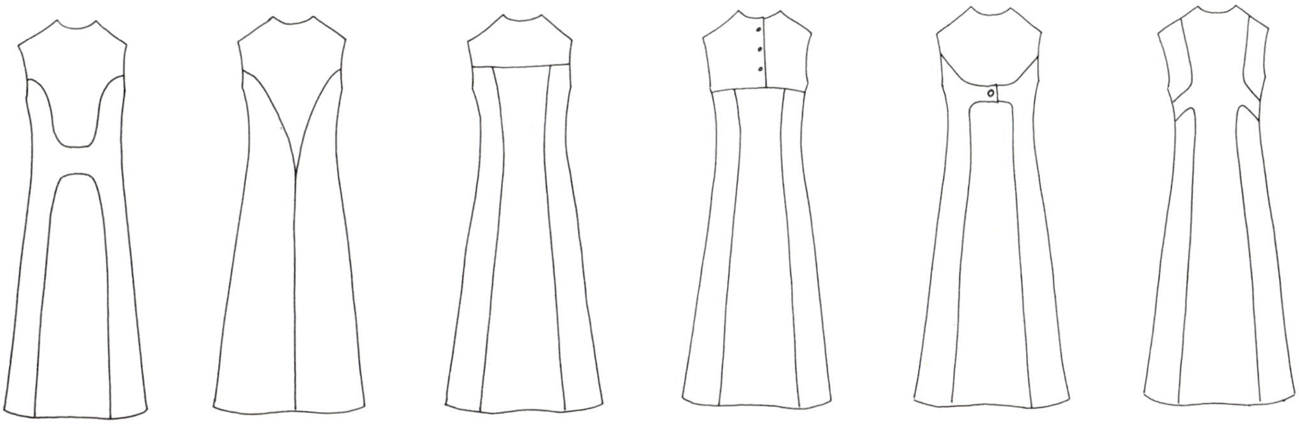

Princess seams should end at the edge of a garment or at the junction of another seam.

French darts, used to shape the A-line silhouette, further extend the range of opportunities for creative seaming.

EXERCISE 2

On Figures 3, 4, and 5, connect the darts to create seams.

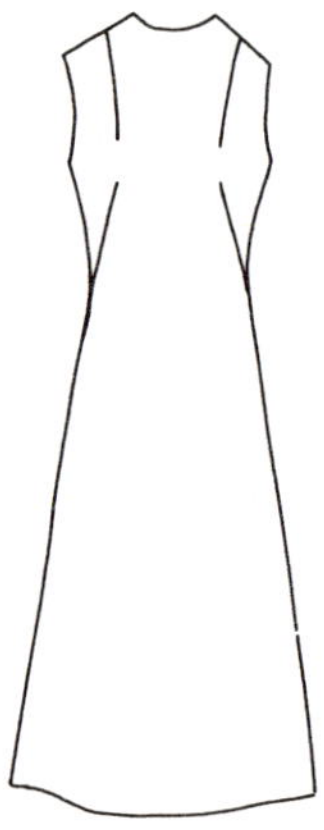

Figure 3

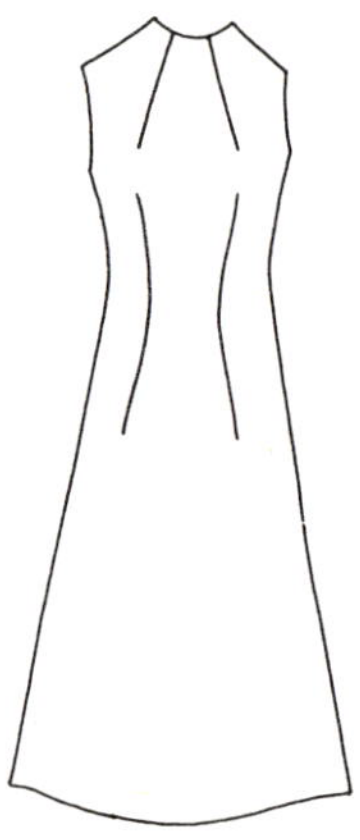

Figure 4

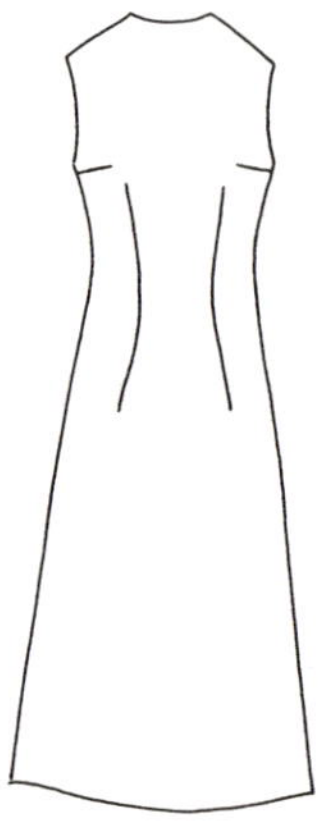

Figure 5

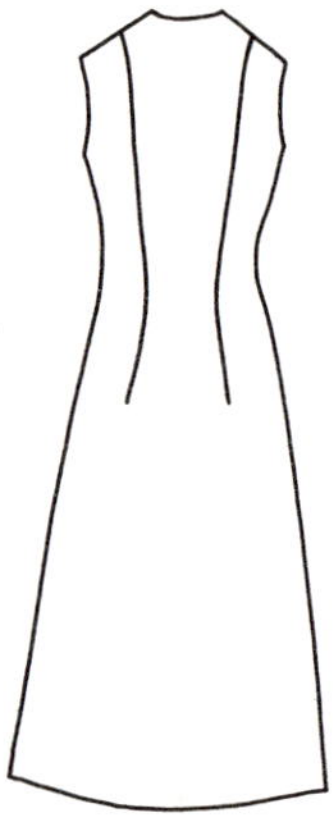

Figure 6. Incorrect
These are still darts because they do not extend to edge of garment.

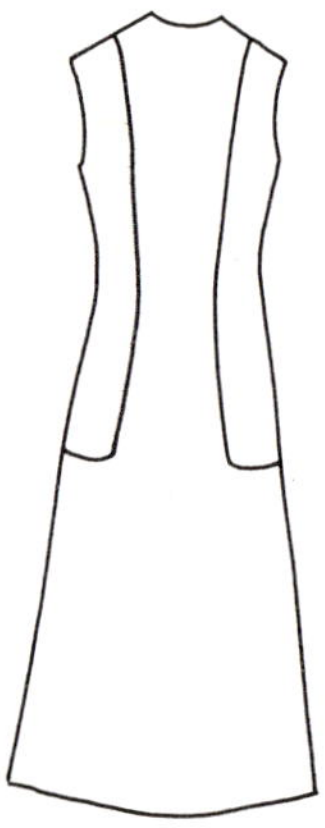

Figure 7. Correct
Seams extend to edge of garment.

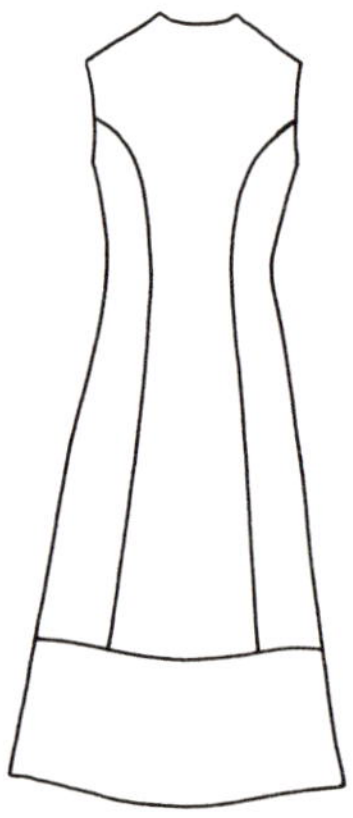

Figure 8. Correct
Seams intersect another seam.

EXERCISE 3

Place a piece of tracing paper over the "thumbnail" figures provided on this page. Draw a princess or A-line silhouette and insert the proper darts. Design eight dresses by connecting these darts in unique and original ways. Remember, unless darts or shirring are used, a seam must intersect or pass through the apex of the bust (see Unit 5, page 39).

These figures are known as *thumbnails*, because they are so small. Rough or unfinished designs are often worked out on thumbnail figures. Sometimes a designer will quickly sketch twenty or thirty designs over them, and then select the best ones, perhaps only four or five, for further use.

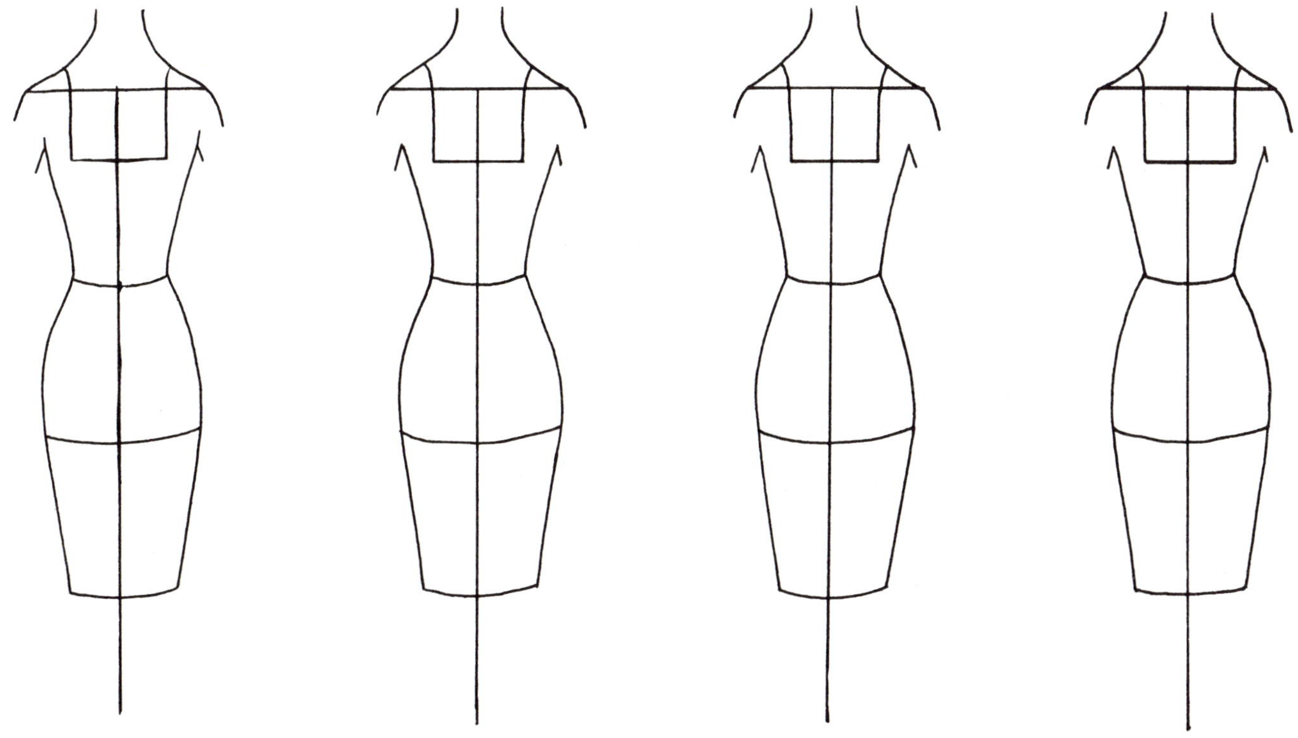

Example 1. Bust, Waist, and Hip Darts

Step 1 Draw silhouette. Step 2 Insert darts. Step 3 Connect darts. Step 4 Finish design.

Example 2. French Darts

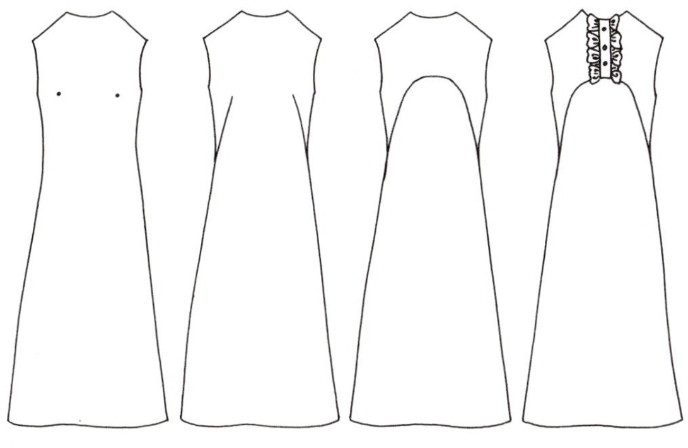

Step 1 Draw silhouette. Step 2 Insert darts. Step 3 Connect darts. Step 4 Finish design.

LESSON FOURTEEN

necklines and seams—how they work together

Now that you are familiar with the technique of designing with seams, it is time to combine that knowledge with what you know about necklines. In Lesson Thirteen, all the princess and A-line illustrations, as well as the dresses you designed, have round necklines. However, there is no rule that requires any dress to have a particular type of neckline. Generally, the seamlines of a dress will influence the design of its neckline, or vice versa—that is, a neckline may also influence the design of a dress.

The seams on the A-line silhouette in Figure 9 were designed before the neckline, which then followed quite naturally.

In Figure 10, the V-shaped neckline was the first design element. Seaming was inspired by the neckline.

Repetition, the principle of design discussed in Unit 2, is the major factor at work here. Notice that in Figure 9 the curved shape of the seam is repeated in the neckline; whereas in Figure 10 the V-shaped neckline is repeated in the seams and once again in the inverted pleat.

EXERCISE 4

Using the thumbnail figures on page 59, redraw without necklines the eight designs completed for Exercise 3.

Redesign each neckline so that its shape in some way conforms to the shapes created by your seamlines.

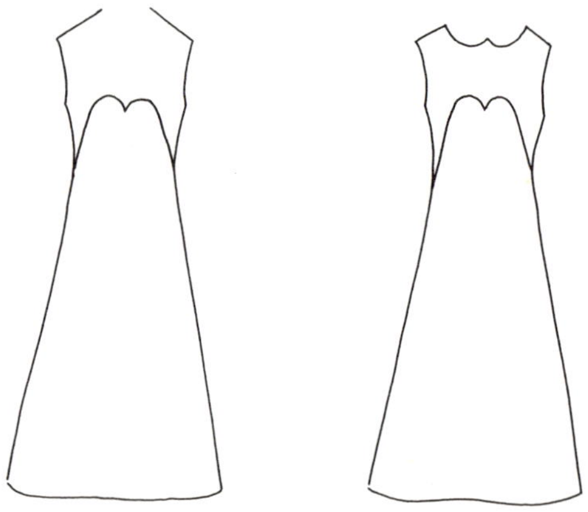

Figure 9

Figure 10

UNIT 9 illustrating an original design in color

LESSON FIFTEEN

VELLUM

EXERCISES 1 AND 2

From Tracing Paper To Vellum

LESSON FIFTEEN

vellum

In Unit 8 you learned how to design with seams and necklines working together. But the eight thumbnail designs completed for Exercise 4 or that unit are still rough sketches. A finished trade sketch is a larger drawing illustrated in color.

Professionals often present their finished designs on vellum, which is heavier and less transparent than tracing paper. A technique frequently employed with the use of vellum calls for colored pencils and fixative spray.

There are several ways to use colored pencils on vellum. The simplest procedure is to color without shadows. More complicated methods involve a knowledge of shading, and will be dealt with in Unit 11.

EXERCISE 1 FROM TRACING PAPER TO VELLUM

1. Select a dress design from one of your eight thumbnail sketches.
2. Redraw that design on tracing paper over a large croqui from Unit 4. Include in this drawing the entire body—hair, face, hands, feet, etc.
3. Perfect this drawing to the best of your ability. Check for common errors: Is the hemline parallel to the hipline? Do the seams intersect the apex of the bust? Do the armholes end above the bustline? (Remember, armholes are higher than bustlines.)
4. On your drawing board, first place a piece of blank white paper; over that the finished tracing-paper sketch; and on top of that a sheet of vellum.
5. When the figure is positioned so that it is in the center of the vellum (not falling over but standing up straight), then secure all three sheets of paper with push pins or masking tape.
6. Trace the complete drawing onto the vellum with a #2H pencil. Use an accented pencil line (study Unit 10, page 72).
7. Spray fixative over this front side of the vellum to keep pencil lines from smearing.
8. Remove the tracing paper, which is no longer needed. Place the sprayed side of the vellum (the side with the drawing on it) facing down on the white paper with the blank side of the vellum facing up.
9. The vellum is now ready to be colored. All coloring is done on the *back side* of the vellum. (The traced drawing facing down is the front side.)
10. With short, even strokes, color the entire figure—skin, hair, dress, shoes, etc. Strive to achieve a smooth, flat, unshaded look. *Do not* color any background.
11. When finished, spray the colored side of the vellum. Do not move it until the spray has dried, or the colors will run.
12. Finished vellums may be mounted in a pad, inserted in plastic folders in a ring binder, or kept for your collection in any other way which neatly displays them.

You have just completed a vellum in color, without the use of shading.

EXERCISE 2 FROM TRACING PAPER TO VELLUM

Select another dress design from your thumbnail sketches, and finish it on vellum as instructed above.

UNIT 10 the use of shadows

LESSON SIXTEEN

TYPES OF SHADING

PENCIL TECHNIQUES

ACCENTED PENCIL LINES

LESSON REVIEW

EXERCISES 1, 2, AND 3

LESSON SEVENTEEN

SHADING THE TRADE SKETCH

LESSON SIXTEEN

the use of shadows

Whenever a professional artist or illustrator begins an assignment, certain questions regarding the artwork arise automatically. For example: What is the purpose of this illustration? Who will see it, and why? Should it be stark and dramatic, or soft and natural? Must it be realistic, or only make suggestions to the imagination? In answering these questions, the illustrator determines his approach to a particular piece of work; and that approach will include, among other things, the way in which shadows are used.

There are dozens of shading techniques, but only a few are necessary for the execution of a trade sketch. So in order to limit ourselves to essentials, we must ask the purpose of a trade sketch. And since its purpose is to demonstrate a garment in a simple but attractive manner, so that construction and design are immediately apparent—then shadows on a trade sketch must be simple, not overbearing or dramatic, and used primarily to clarify the costume.

TYPES OF SHADING

Three things are true of all shadows, no matter what technique an artist employs, or the purpose of his work.

1. The *shape* of a shadow is determined by the shape of an object. If an object is round, then its shadow must reflect that roundness. Shadows describe and mold shapes.

Correct

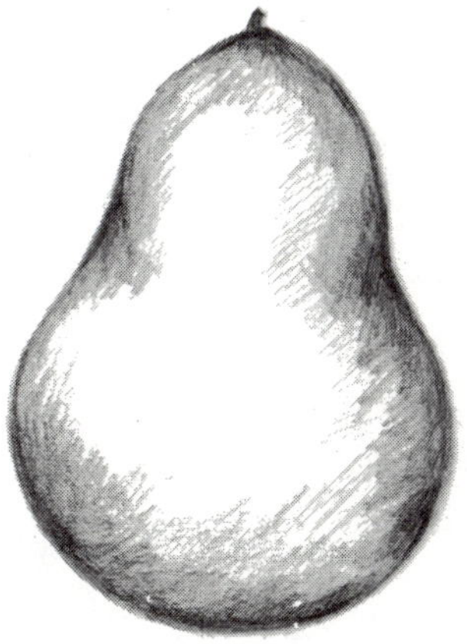

Correct

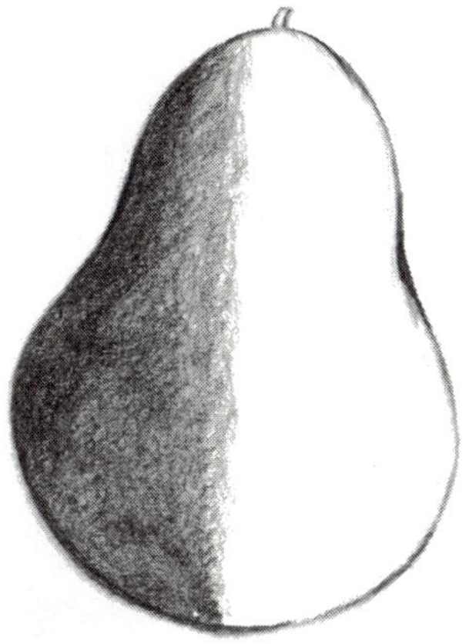

Incorrect

2. The *position* or *placement* of a shadow is determined by a source of light. The deepest shadows are furthest away from the light.

Light hitting from the right.

Light hitting from the top.

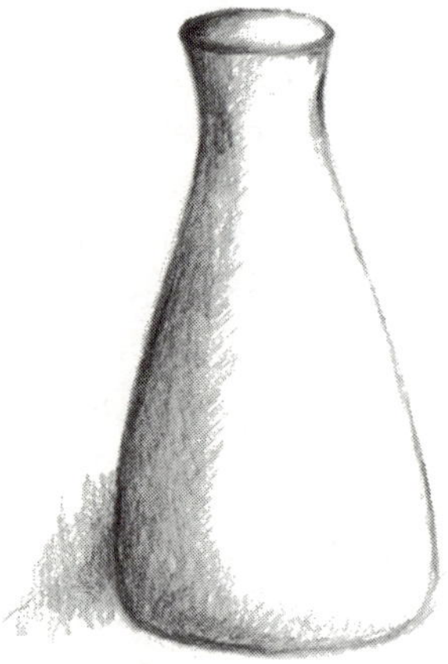

Light hitting from the left.

3. Depending upon the way an object is situated, and the source of its lighting, it will more or less cast shadows *behind* it.

Shadows behind apples.

Folds in fabric cast shadows behind them.

We have just seen that all shadows have shapes which reflect the shape of an object; that the position or placement of shadows is determined by a source of light; and that sometimes an object or thing will cast its shadow upon something else.

But many other qualities of shadows are changeable, or depend entirely upon an artist's interpretation. For example: shadows can be made to appear stark and dramatic, or soft and subtle.

DRAMATIC—If a shadow does not range from light to dark, but is instead limited to one or a few values, then the effect is dramatic. The darker the shadow, the more dramatic its effect.

Dramatic

NATURAL—If a shadow moves gradually from light to dark, its appearance is softer and quite natural.

Natural

PENCIL TECHNIQUES

Pencil technique influences the appearance of a sketch, and may create a mood or feeling.

Crosshatch pencil technique

CROSSHATCH—First a layer of pencil lines is applied, with all the lines drawn in one direction. The second layer of lines crosses those of the first layer, creating what appears to be a deepening shadow.

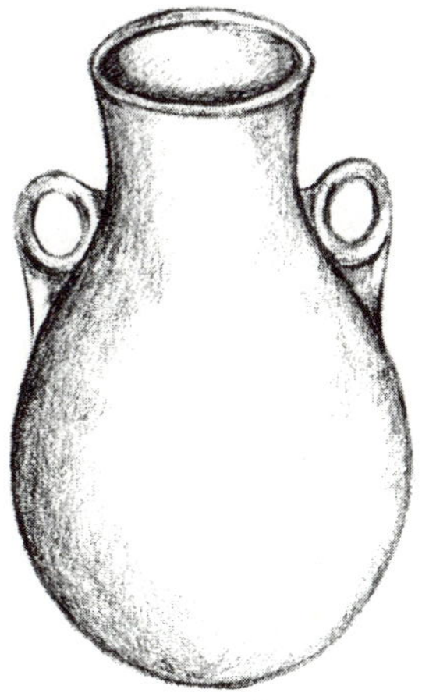

Smooth and blended pencil technique

SMOOTH AND BLENDED—This technique requires no rubbing (limited to charcoal), but is achieved through the slow and patient application of layers of shadow carefully blended one into the other.

ACCENTED PENCIL LINES

Just as there are various kinds of pencil techniques employed in shading, so also are there different kinds of lines. The accented line is the most popular with fashion illustrators, and is used consistently on trade sketches. An accented line goes from light to dark and thin to thick. It gets thicker and darker:

1. where there are indentations on the edge of an object;
2. where shadows fall;
3. or any other place the artist wishes to accentuate part of a drawing with a stronger line.

LESSON REVIEW

1. The shape of a shadow is determined by the shape of an object.
2. The placement of a shadow is determined by a source of light.
3. Depending upon position and source of light, some things will more or less cast shadows behind them.
4. Artists determine the appearance of shadows by manipulating lights and darks, pencil technique, and line. Soft and gradual shadows and a crosshatch or smooth, blended look are used in trade sketching, together with the accented line.

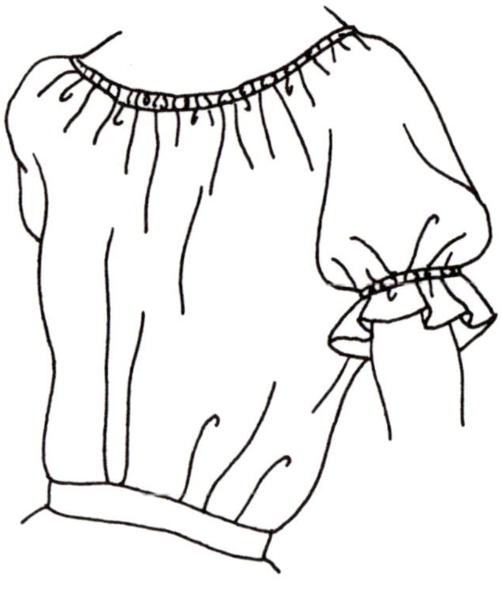
Not accented (contour line)

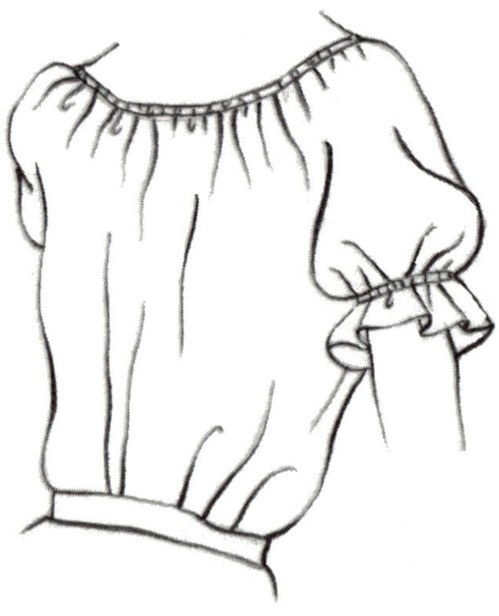
Accented

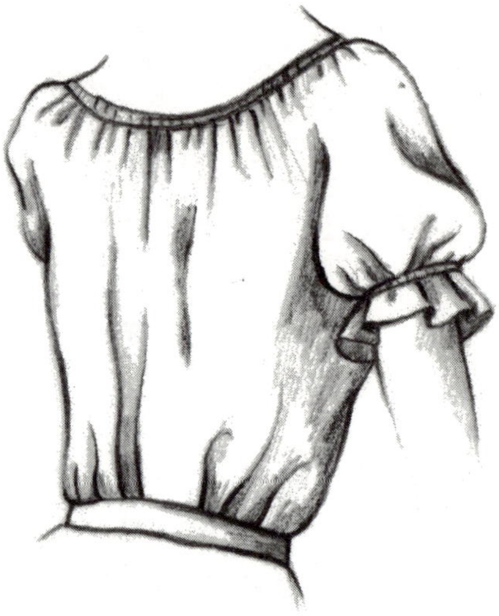
Shading with accented line.

EXERCISE 1

Place a piece of sketching paper over the objects illustrated here and trace them. Pretend that light is hitting them either on the left or right. Using a #2 or HB pencil, shade each object on its opposite side—the side away from the light, the side in shadow.

NOTE In examining your work, look for the following:

1. Do the shadows reflect the shapes of the objects?
2. Are the darkest shadows furthest away from the light?

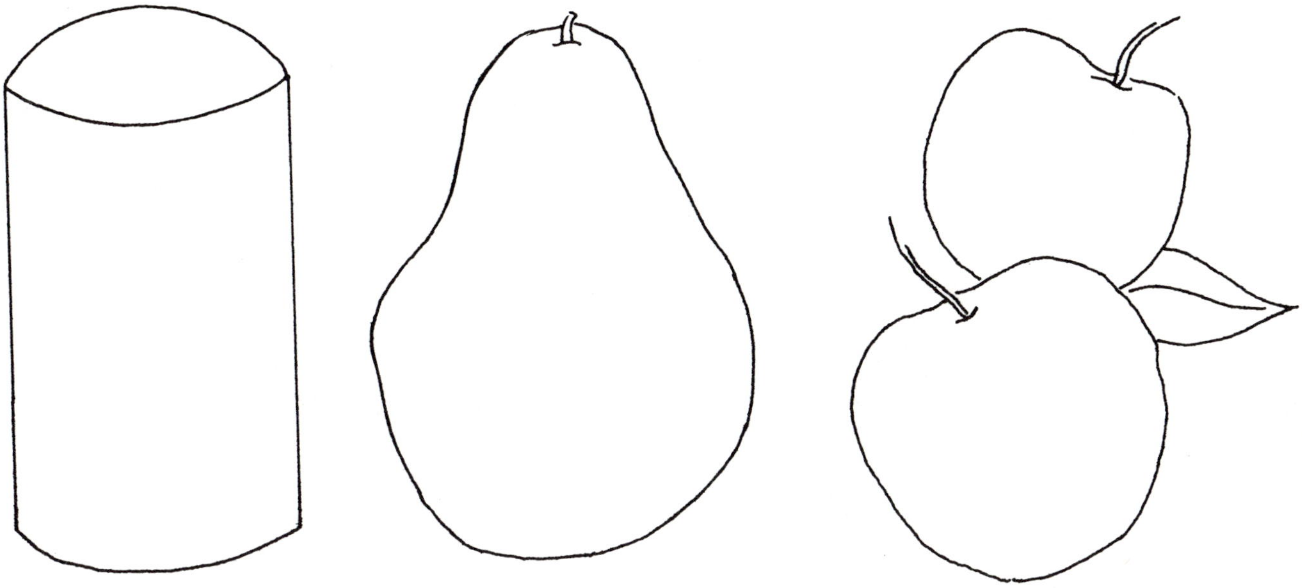

EXERCISE 2

For the purposes of trade sketching, soft and subtle shadows are preferable to dramatic ones. Therefore, each shadow must begin almost invisibly, and get darker *very* gradually.

Place a piece of sketching paper over the above shapes and trace them. Concentrate on creating a shadow that becomes darker very gradually. Use a crosshatch pencil technique (see page 71).

EXERCISE 3

Set up a still life with two pieces of fruit, one behind the other. Draw and then shade it, using a smooth and blended pencil technique. Finish with an accented line.

NOTE The object in front should cast a shadow upon the one behind it.

LESSON SEVENTEEN

shading the trade sketch

Shadows on a trade sketch are used to point out the construction and design of a garment, and also to add some roundness to the figure.

Shadows on the A-line skirt, Figure 1, accomplish several things:

1. They suggest the movement of the body, and also indicate a light source on the right.
2. If the light hits on the right, then the opposite side of each leg will be in shadow. Simple shading on the left side of each leg creates an illusion of roundness.

Shadows on the fitted blouse, Figure 2, indicate a light source on the left. Therefore, while the right side of the body is shaded, the right side of each arm is also in shadow. Other shadows fall in folds, and below the collar; and tend to mold the shape of the body.

Figure 1.
A-line Skirt

Figure 2.
Fitted Blouse

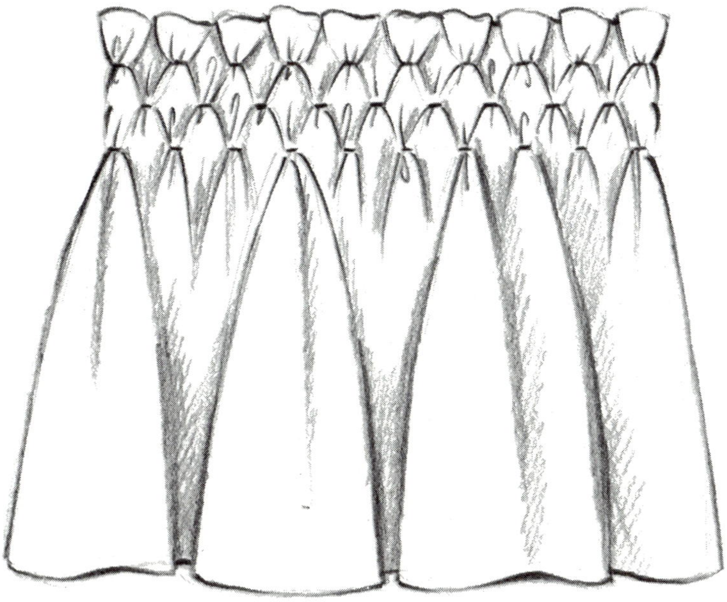

Figure 3. Smocking
Shadows fall behind folds and in recesses. The closer to the fold, the darker the shadow.

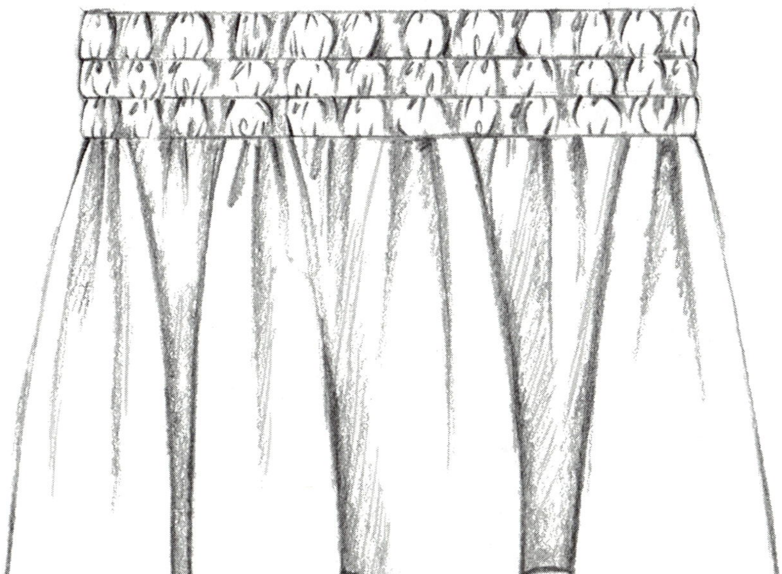

Figure 4. Shirring

Figure 5.
Gathered Skirt with Ruffle
Shadows fall behind folds and on left side of legs, indicating a light source on the right.

Figure 6. Flares
Shadows come to a point and disappear at the top of flares; darkest areas fall directly behind flares.

Figure 7.
Sleeve with Flares
Light source on the left.

Figure 8.
Skirt with Flares
Light source on the right.

UNIT 11
shading on vellum

LESSON EIGHTEEN

COMPLETE COLORING TECHNIQUE

EXERCISE 1

LESSON NINETEEN

PARTIAL COLORING TECHNIQUE

EXERCISE 2

Figure 1.
Complete Coloring Technique

Figure 2.
Partial Coloring Technique

Figure 2.
Partial Coloring Technique

Figure 1.
Complete Coloring Technique

LESSON EIGHTEEN

complete coloring technique

Unit 10, Lesson Seventeen, presented examples of shading as it should appear on a trade sketch. With vellum, this type of shading is used in two ways—as part of a complete or a partial coloring technique (see Figures 1 and 2, page 79).

EXERCISE 1

1. Transfer a finished drawing to a sheet of vellum, using an accented pencil line. Spray the front side with fixative.

2. Turn vellum over and color the entire drawing on the wrong side, just as you did before. But this time, use your colored pencils lightly, so that when shading, darker tones can be achieved by applying more pressure.

3. Select colors for shadows:
   SKIN Whatever the basic skin color, use a brown pencil for shading.
   HAIR Blonde, red, or light brown—use brown for shading. Dark brown or black—use black.
   CLOTHES The important thing to remember is that shadows are darker than the original color. Therefore, it is sometimes necessary to use more than one pencil when shading. For example, when starting with a medium-green color, a darker green pencil must be used for shading. If more pressure were applied to the medium-green pencil, the color would be greener, but not necessarily darker. If, however, a colored pencil gets darker when pressure is applied, then the same pencil may be used for shading. Most dark colors (navy blue, purple, wine, dark green, etc.) work this way, if used lightly for the basic coloring.

4. Begin to shade. Pretend that light is hitting the figure on the right. The left side of each arm and leg will therefore have some shadow. The left side of the body should be more shaded than the right. Shadows must mold the shape, appearing on the face, under the chin, around the bust, on the skirt; and also under belts, pockets, flaps, etc. Work with a tissue beneath your palm to prevent smearing.

5. Remove all smudges with a kneaded eraser.

6. Spray colored side of vellum.

LESSON NINETEEN

partial coloring technique

A partial coloring technique is simple, speedy, and effective when properly applied. Its use, however, requires a thorough knowledge of shading, since coloring is limited to areas where shadows normally fall.

EXERCISE 2

Complete a vellum using a partial coloring technique. This is a fast method, so strive to finish the illustration in approximately ten minutes. Time yourself.

UNIT 12 designing skirts

LESSON TWENTY

pleats

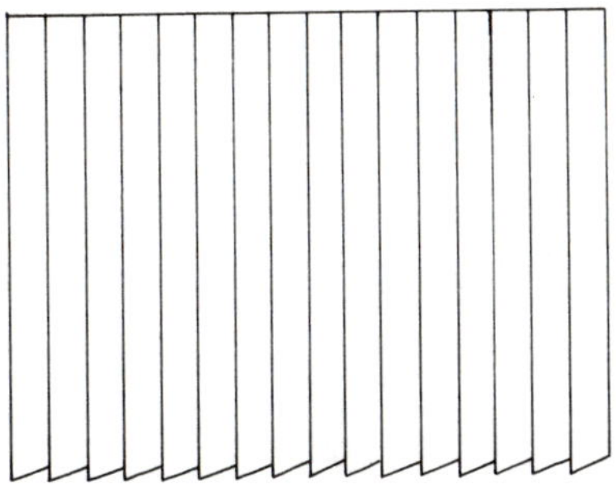

Side Pleats

Box Pleats

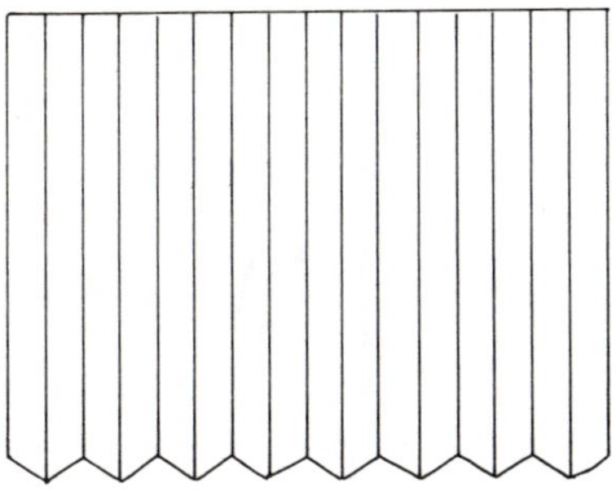

Accordion Pleats

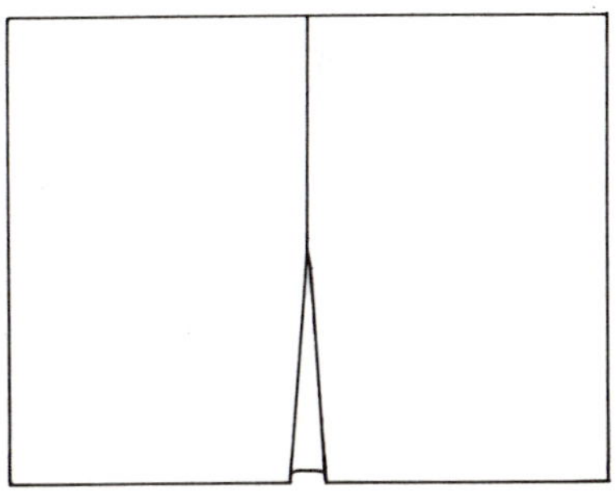

Inverted Pleat

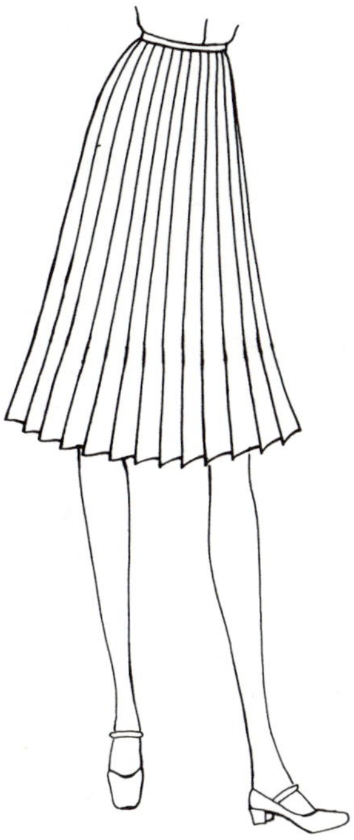

Side Pleats

Box Pleats

Accordion Pleats

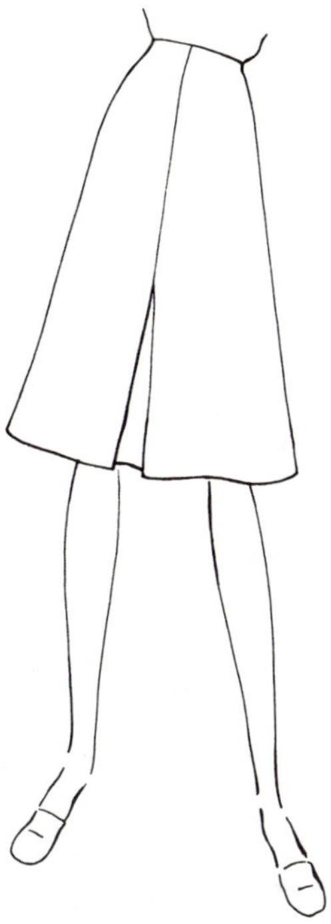

Inverted Pleat

DRAWING PLEATS

Pleats are drawn wider at the hemline than at the waistline. This is easily accomplished by dividing the waistline and hemline into halves, quarters, eighths, and so on, until obtaining the desired number of pleats.

Example 1. Front View

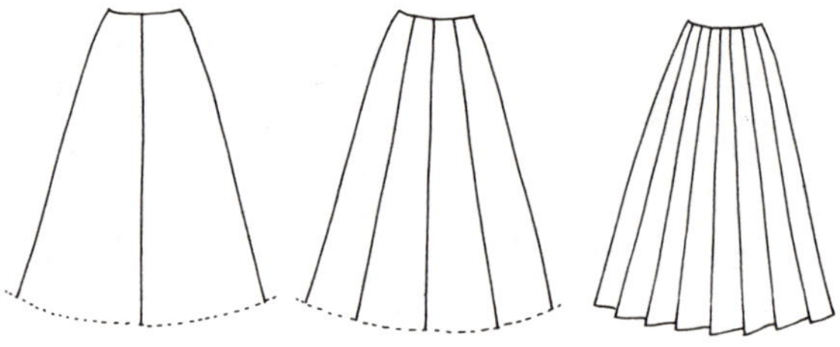

Step 1 Draw center line. Step 2 Divide into quarters. Step 3 Continue dividing.

Example 2. Three-Quarter View

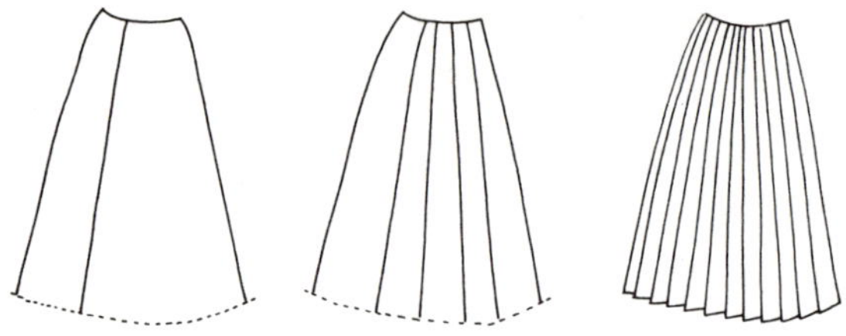

Step 1 Draw center line

Step 2 Divide into quarters, eighths, etc., on the large side only. Fill in remaining pleats on small side. Do not "squeeze"—pleats should be of equal size.

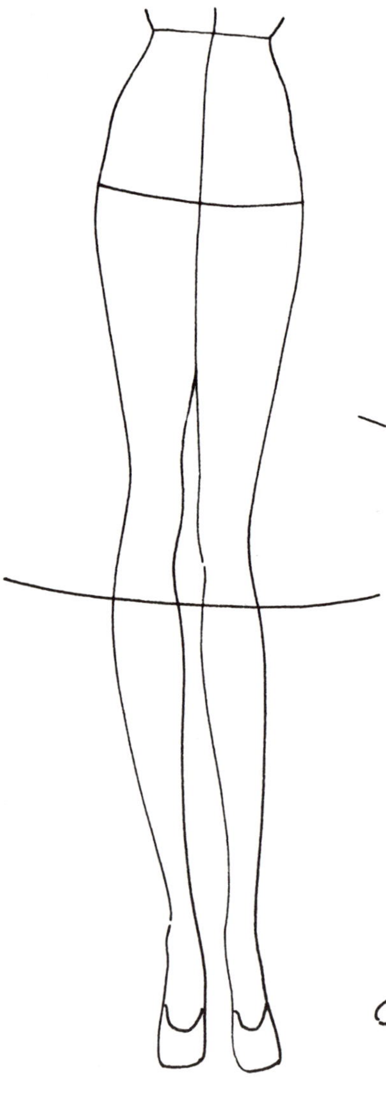

Figure 1

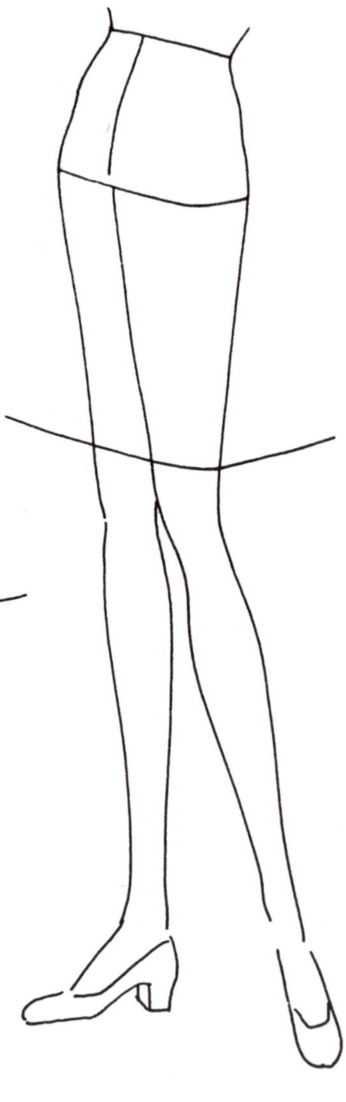

Figure 2

EXERCISE 1

Place a piece of tracing paper over Figure 1. Draw two skirts, one with accordion pleats, and the other with box pleats.

EXERCISE 2

Place a piece of tracing paper over Figure 2. Draw a skirt with an inverted pleat, then one with side pleats.

NOTE The center line on a three-quarter figure is not in the middle.

LESSON TWENTY-ONE

flares

Flares are formed when a circular piece of fabric, narrower at the top than at the bottom, falls into folds.

Skirts with flares are generally circular-cut skirts. The fuller the circle, the greater the number of folds.

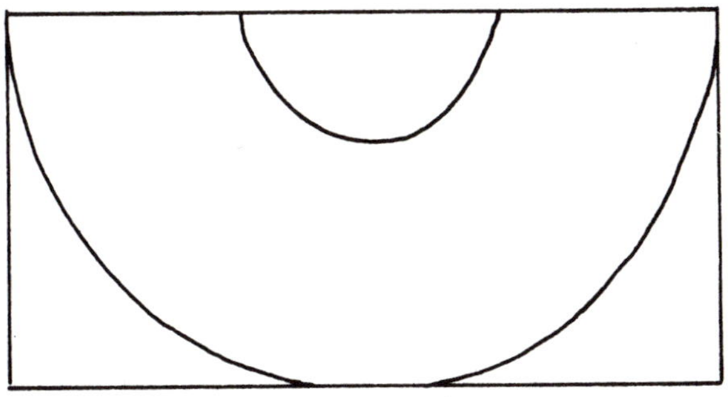

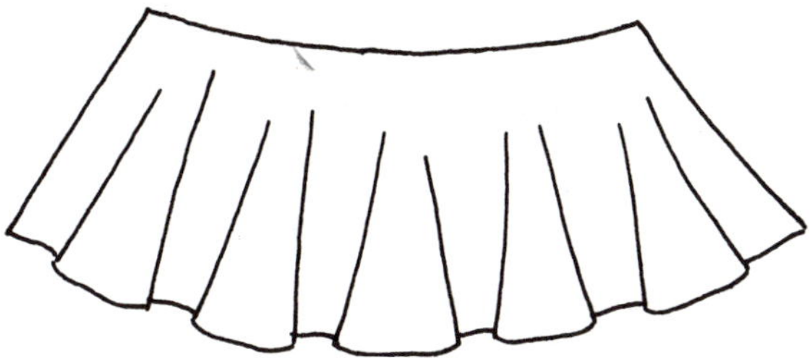

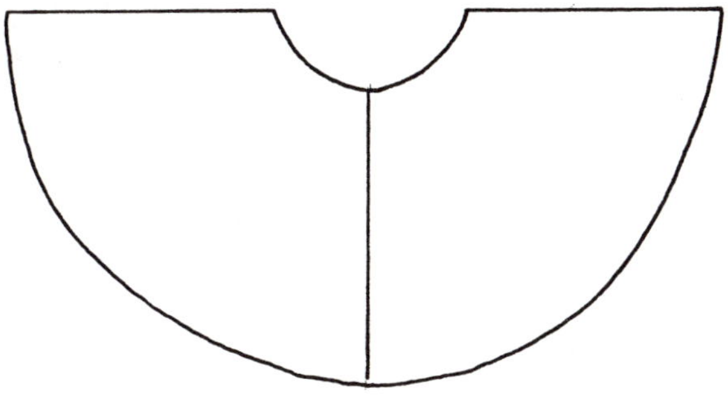

Half Circle Flare

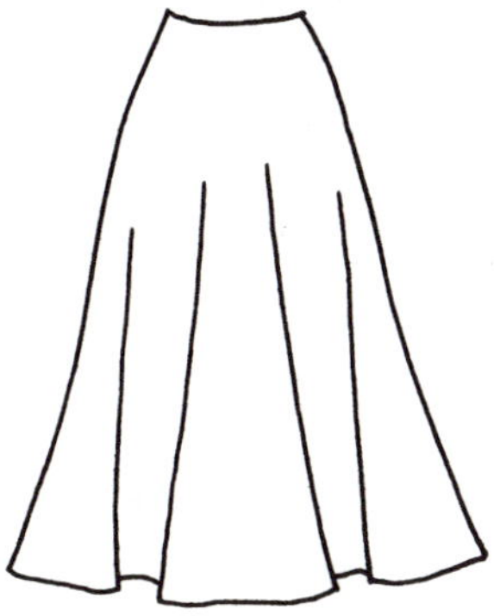

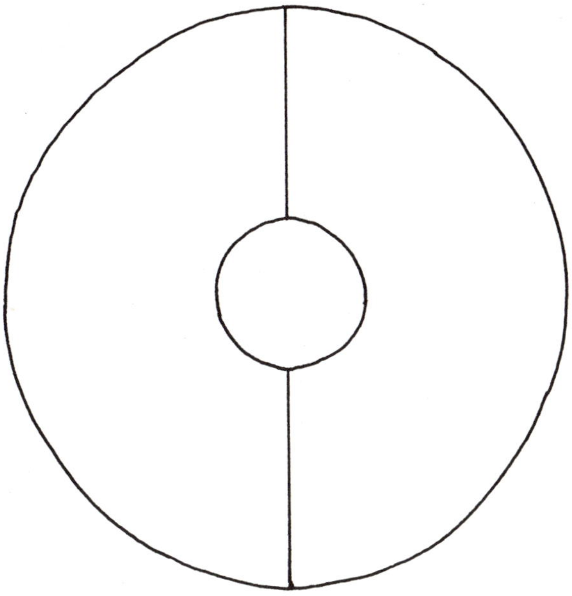

Full Circle Flare

LESSON TWENTY-TWO

combining pleats, flares, stitching, seams

Pleats, flares, stitching, and seaming may be combined in diverse ways for interesting effects. The use of belts, pockets, and other trimming further expands the range of design possibilities.

EXERCISE 3

Place a piece of tracing paper over a front-view croqui. Design five pleated skirts with stitching or seaming detail (see page 20).

EXERCISE 4

On a piece of tracing paper over a front-view croqui, design five skirts with flares. Vary them with the use of stitching, seaming, pockets, belts, or other types of trimming. Refer to a book on the history of costume for design ideas.

EXERCISE 5

Select a few of your best designs. Illustrate designs on vellum, using the complete coloring technique.

UNIT 13 designing for summer

LESSON TWENTY-THREE

VARIATIONS OF THE BASIC SILHOUETTES

EXERCISE 1

LESSON TWENTY-THREE

variations of the basic silhouettes

Unit 6 was devoted to basic silhouettes and their construction. In Unit 8 you designed variations of the princess and A-line silhouettes by creating interesting seamlines. In addition to seaming, other elements may be used to vary the basic silhouettes. Among them are flares, pleats, shirring, smocking, and trimming.

These illustrations of summer dresses combine basic silhouettes with those design elements.

Figure 1.
Blouson Variation with Flares

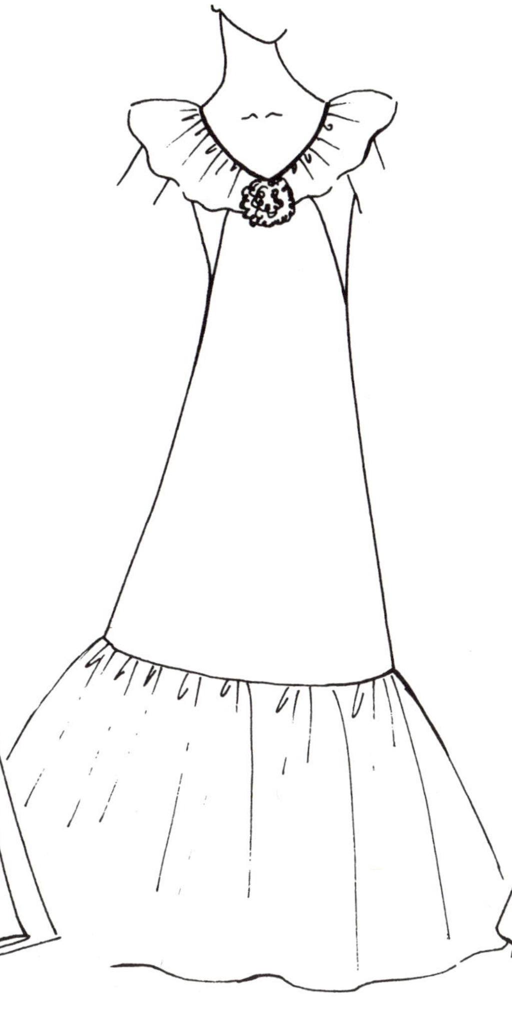

Figure 2.
A-line with Ruffles

Figure 3.
Chemise with Pleats

In addition, each dress utilizes one of the basic necklines discussed in Unit 7, so that collars (and also sleeves) are not essential to their design.

Figure 4.
Fitted Waist with Smocking and Shirring

Figure 5.
Empire with Flower Appliqué

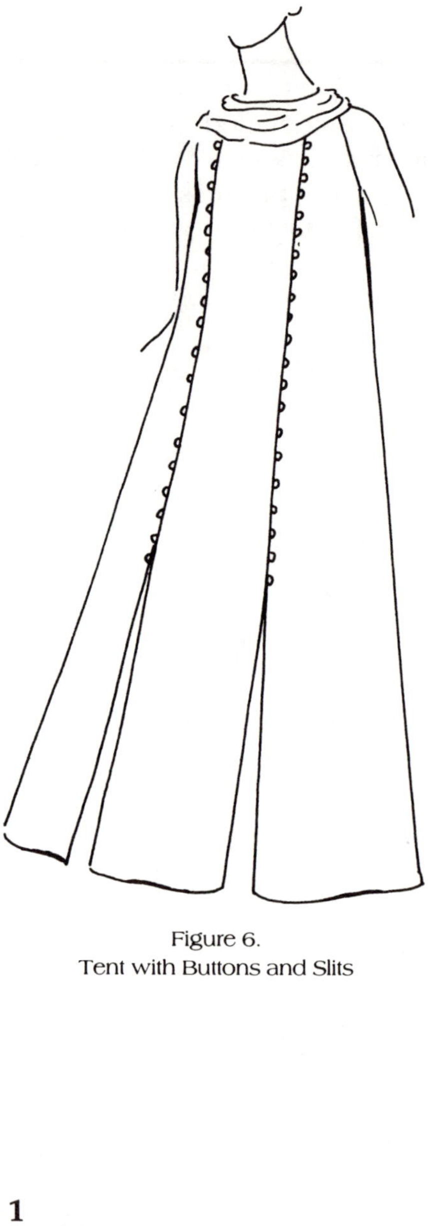

Figure 6.
Tent with Buttons and Slits

EXERCISE 1

Limit your designing for this project to sleeveless dresses without collars. Collars and sleeves will be dealt with in Units 15 and 16.

The most basic silhouettes are the fitted waist, princess, A-line, shift, chemise, tent, blouson, sheath, and empire. Design two dresses for each one, varying them with pleats, shirring, smocking, or trimming.

Use tracing paper over a thumbnail croqui.

UNIT 14 the three-quarter-view fashion figure

LESSON TWENTY-FOUR

developing the three-quarter-view croqui

Although some similarities exist between the procedures for undressing front- and three-quarter view figures, there are important *differences* that must be observed.

Before reading the following instructions, study pages 97 and 99.

UNDRESSING THE THREE-QUARTER-VIEW FIGURE (Developing the Croqui)

1. A three-quarter-view figure is partially turned, so that one side of the body shows more than the other. That part which is turned away seems smaller, and will be referred to as the *small side*. The part which is closer to the viewer, and seems larger, will be called the *large side*.
2. Cut a three-quarter figure out of a pattern book or newspaper. Place this clipping on your drawing board with a sheet of tracing paper over it and secure with push pins or masking tape. Make sure that the figure is standing up straight, and not tilting over.
3. Trace the parts of the body that are not covered by clothing, such as the face, neck, arms, hands, legs, etc.
4. Connect the neck to the outside edge of arms. On the large side of the figure only, draw the inside edge of the arm as high as the armpit.
5. Analyze the figure. Does it have a high hip and low shoulder? This will influence horizontal (those which go across) lines.
6. Draw all the horizontal lines in the following order:
   BUSTLINE Through the apex (fullest part of the bust).
   SHOULDERLINE Parallel to the bustline. On the three-quarter figure the shoulderline goes from the tip of the shoulder on the small side of the figure to a point lower down on the large side (see page 97).

WAISTLINE The lowest point is at the center line. From there, it curves up slightly on either side.

HEMLINE Follow hemline of garment.

HIPLINE Approximately where legs start, parallel to the hemline. Both the hipline and hemline generally curve up slightly close to the edge of the large side.

7. Draw all the vertical lines (those which go up and down).

   THE SIDES OF THE BODY Starting at the armhole on the small side of the figure, draw the side of the body. The bust always protrudes in the direction toward which the figure is turning.

   Draw the other side of the body—always in at the waistline and out again below it.

   THE CENTER LINE Not in the middle of the figure—about a quarter distant from the edge of the small side, and about three-quarters distant from the edge of the large side.

   A. The more the figure is turned away from you, the closer the center line will be to the edge of the body on the small side.
   B. This line goes from the shoulderline to the hipline, where it then becomes the inside of the leg on the large side of the figure.
   C. Use the center of the collars, buttons, belts, etc., as a guide for placing the center line.

   THE SHOULDER-DART LINES:

   A. Divide in half the distance between the center line and the edge of the shoulderline on the large side of the body only. From there, draw a line down to the bustline, parallel to the center line.
   B. On the small side of the body, the shoulder-dart line is placed at a distance from the center line which is slightly less than on the large side.

The Three-Quarter View Fashion Figure

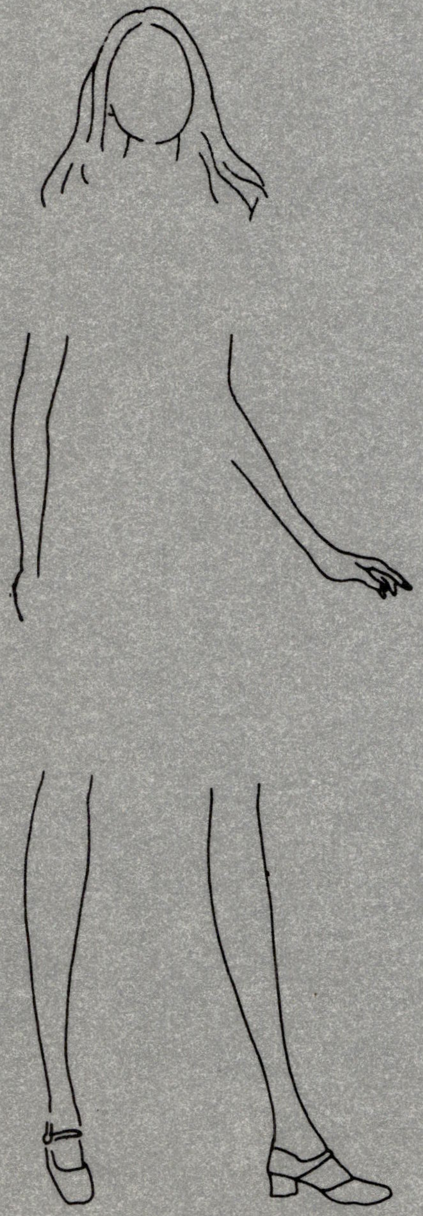

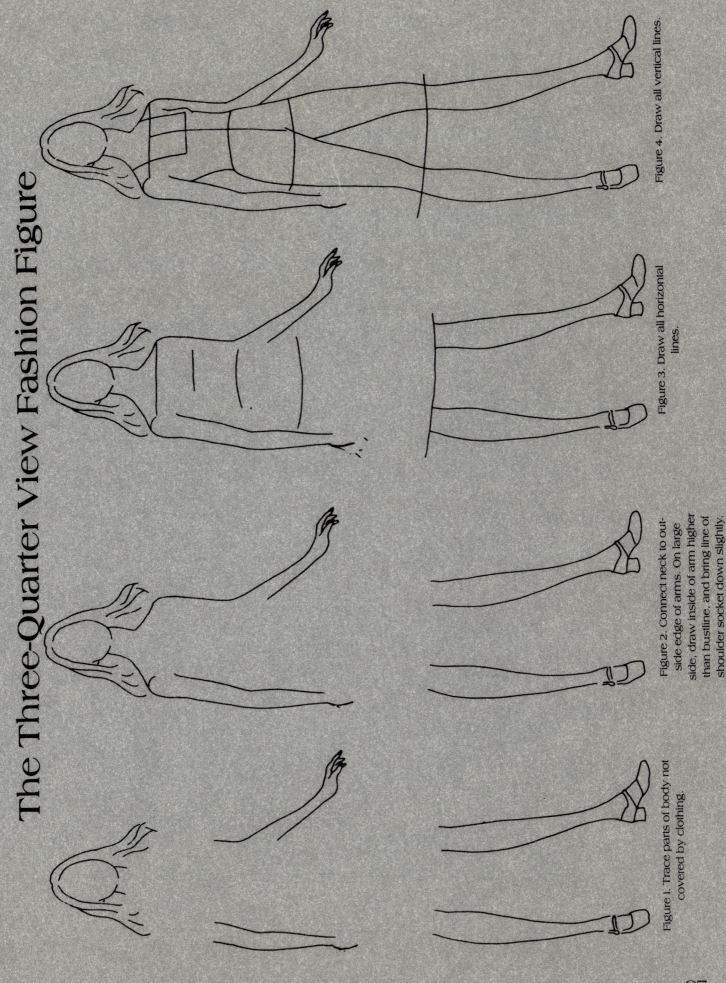

Figure 1. Trace parts of body not covered by clothing.

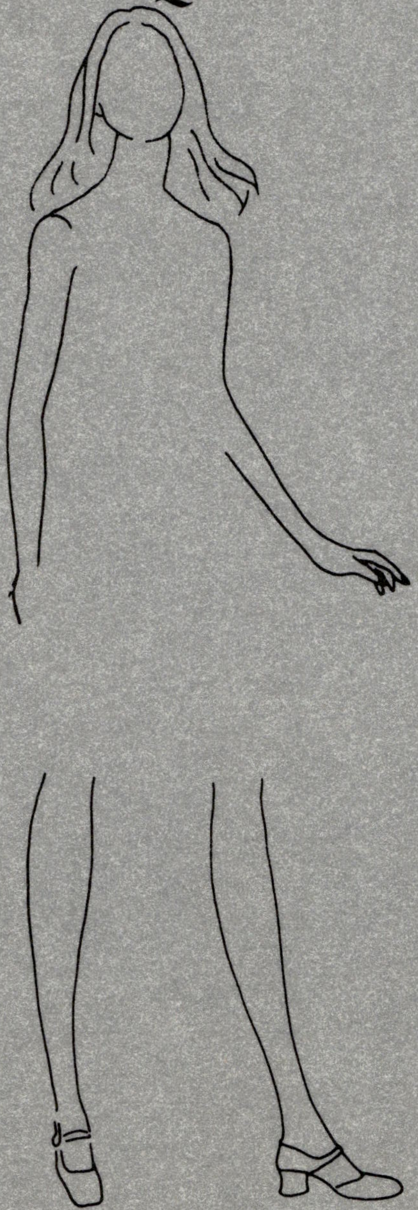

Figure 2. Connect neck to outside edge of arms. On large side, draw inside of arm higher than bustline, and bring line of shoulder socket down slightly.

Figure 3. Draw all horizontal lines.

Figure 4. Draw all vertical lines.

The Three-Quarter View Fashion Figure

Figure 1. Trace parts of body not covered by clothing

Figure 2. Connect neck to outside edge of arms. On large side, draw inside of arm higher than bustline, and bring line of shoulder socket down slightly.

Figure 3. Draw all horizontal lines.

Figure 4. Draw all vertical lines.

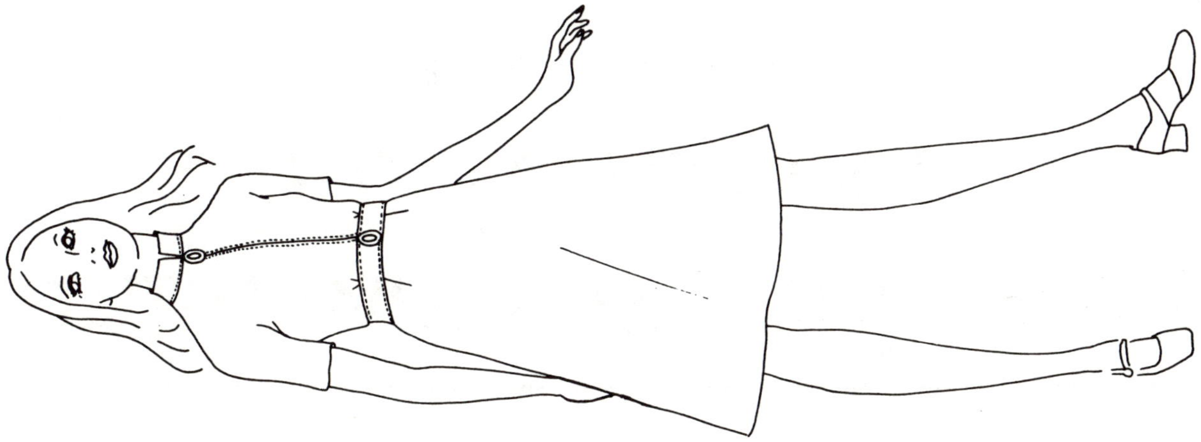
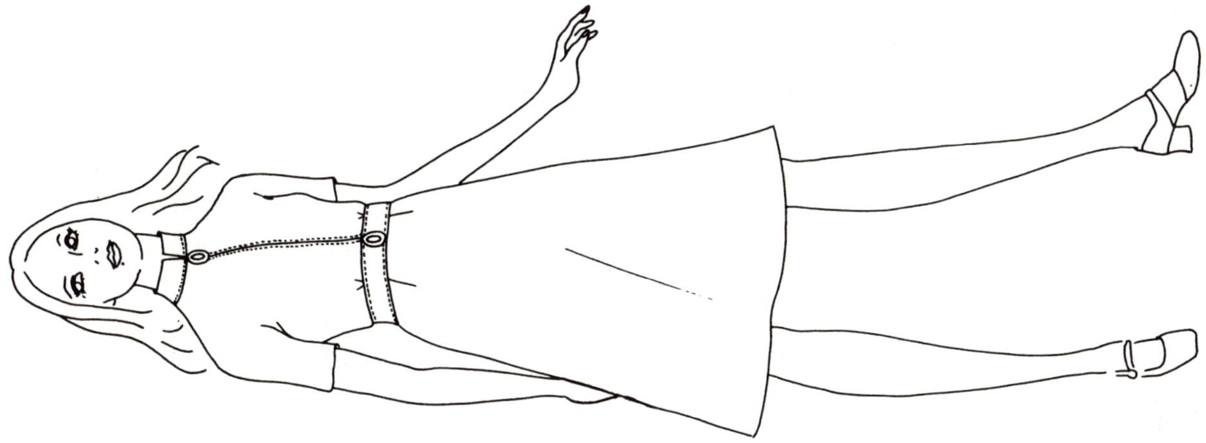
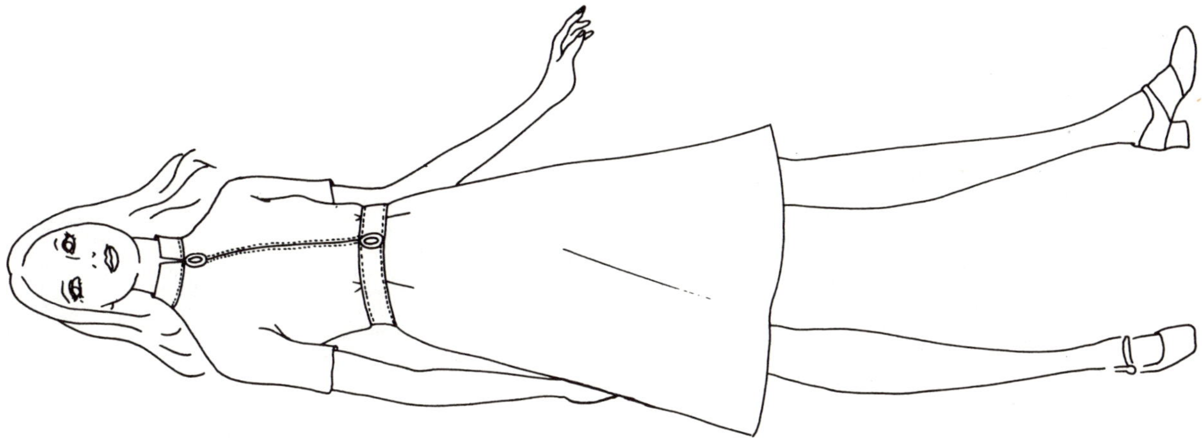
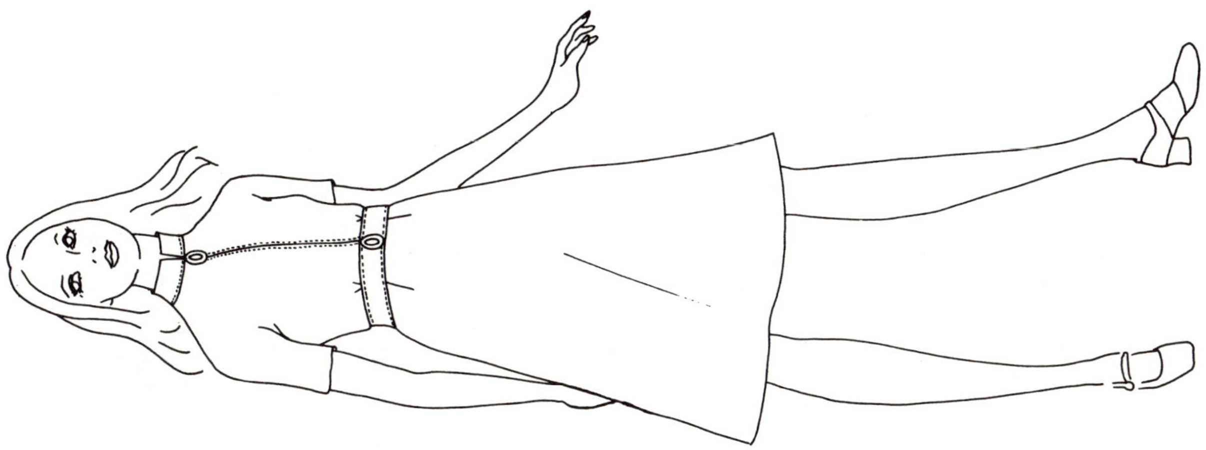

LESSON TWENTY-FIVE

undressing the three-quarter-view figure

On the following pages are two three-quarter-view fashion figures. Each one is illustrated both dressed and undressed. Complete Exercises 1 and 2 according to the instructions in Lesson Twenty-four.

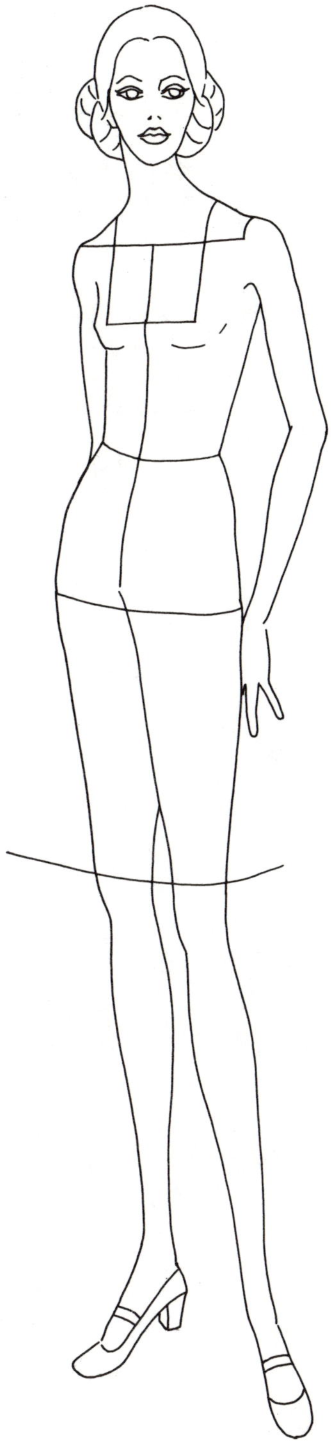

Figure 1. Undressed

Figure 2. Dressed

EXERCISE 1

You may correct your undressed figure by placing it over this one and checking for mistakes.

Place a sheet of tracing paper over this figure and secure with masking tape. Undress according to instructions on pages 94 and 95.

Figure 3. Dressed

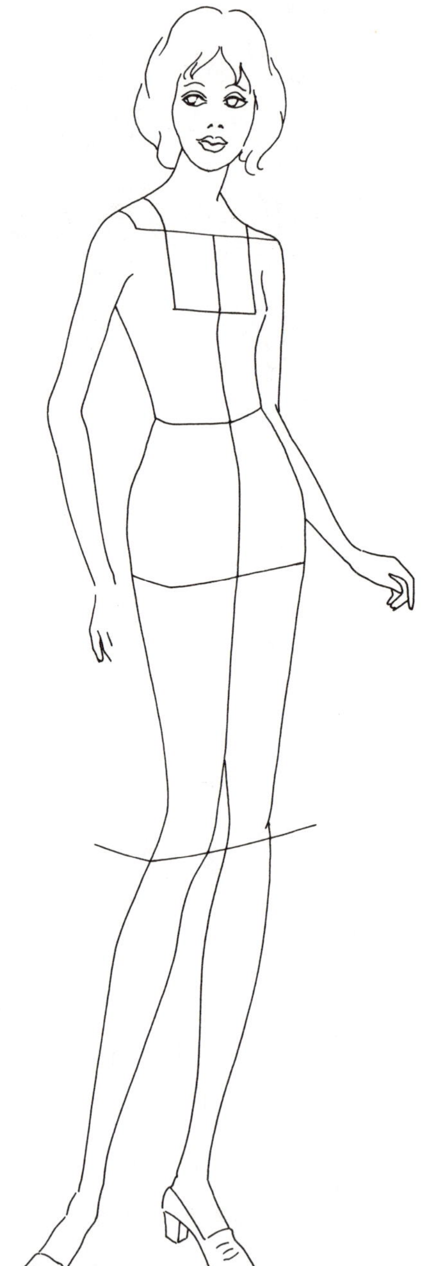

Figure 4. Undressed

EXERCISE 2

Place a sheet of tracing paper over this figure and secure with masking tape. Undress according to instructions on pages 94 and 95.

You may correct your undressed figure by placing it over this one and checking for mistakes.

UNIT 15 basic collars

LESSON TWENTY-SIX

basic collars on basic necklines

A collar is constructed upon a neckline, so that many have round or V-shaped bases, and may be either flat or rolled. Although rolled collars are much more difficult to make and sew, requiring complex patternmaking techniques, they are extremely popular and widely used. The following illustrations are the most basic collar types.

Collars on Round Necklines

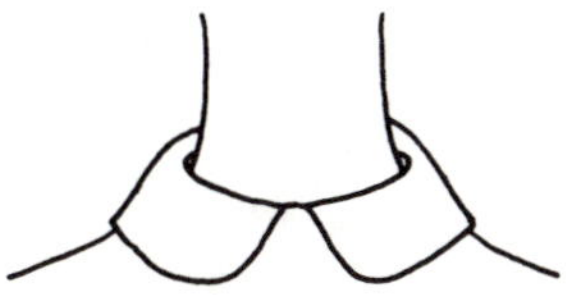

Peter Pan Collar

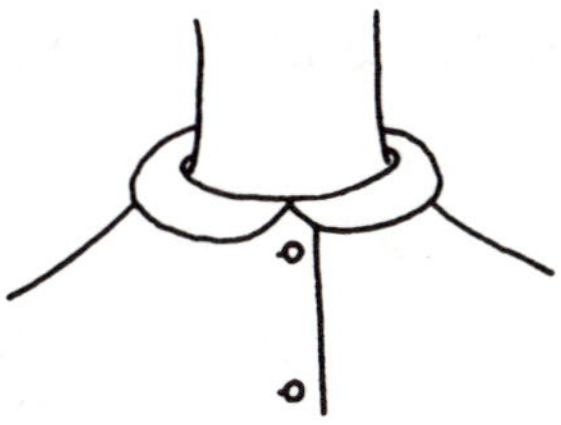

Bobbie Collar

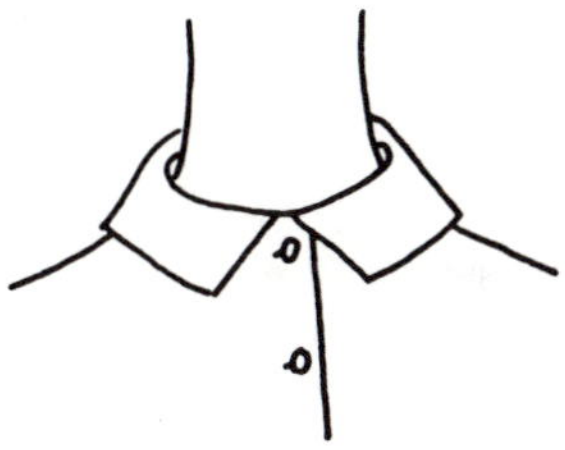

Spread Collar

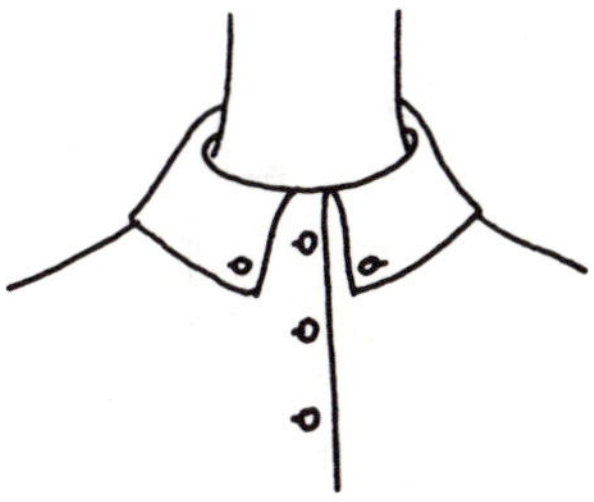

Button-down Collar

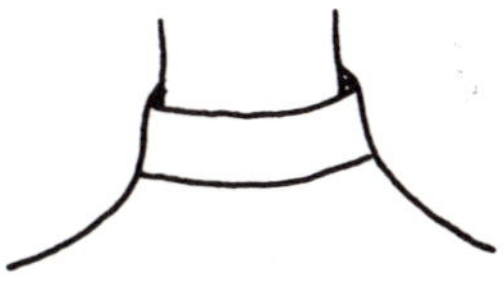

Clerical Collar

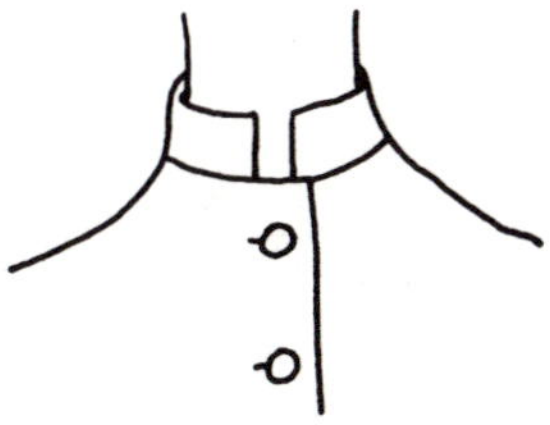

Mandarin Collar

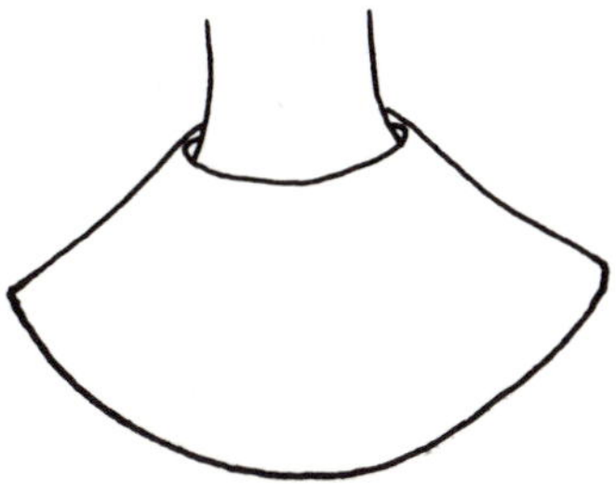

Bertha Collar

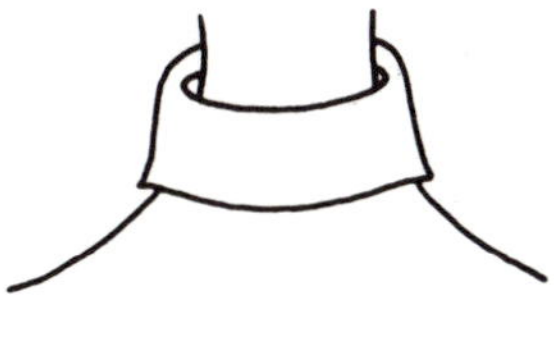

Turtleneck

Collars on V-shaped Necklines

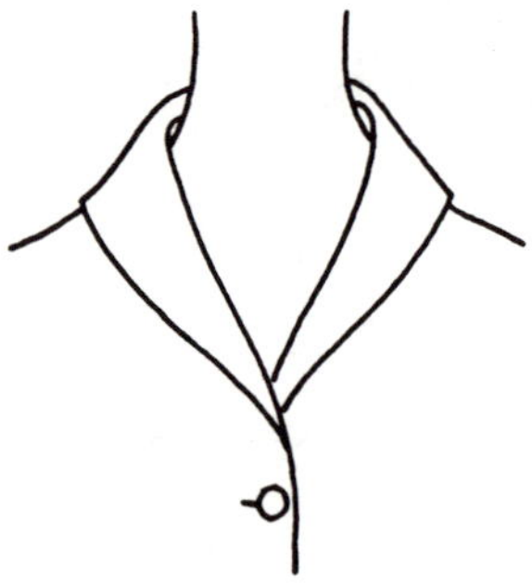

Shawl
Collar

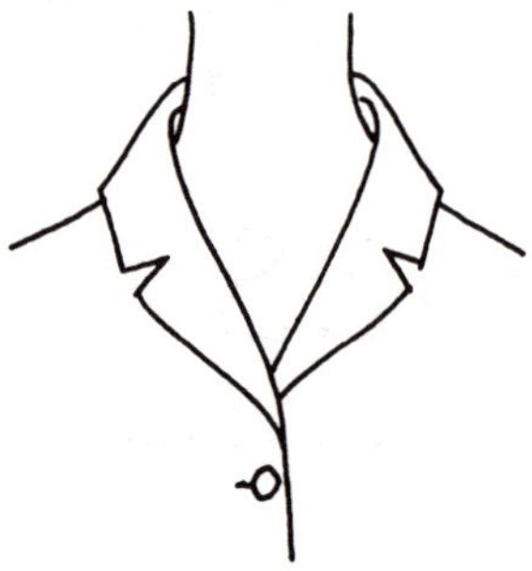

Notched
Collar

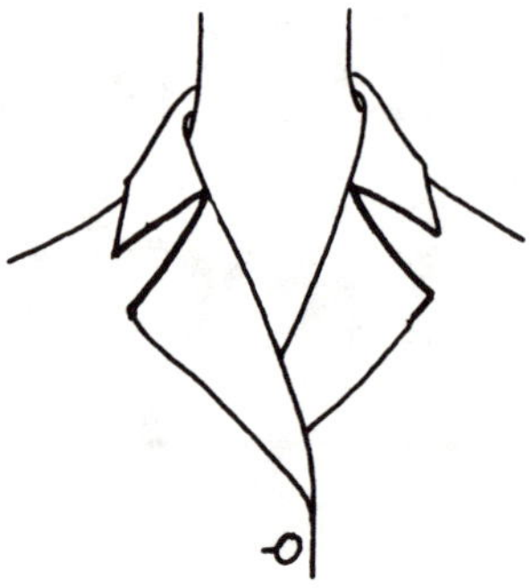

Convertible
Collar

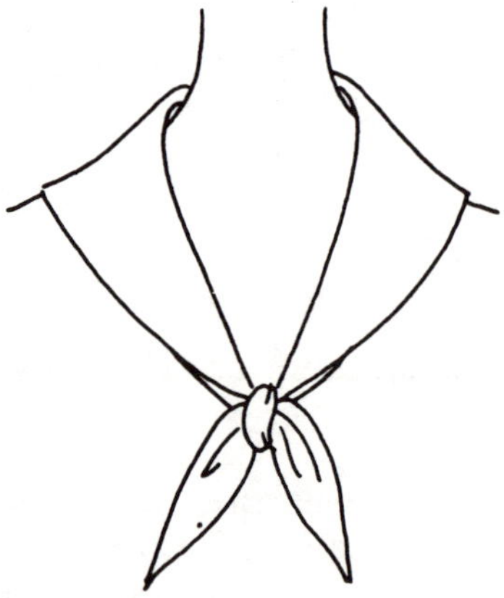

Sailor
Collar

Collars on Boat and Scoop Necklines

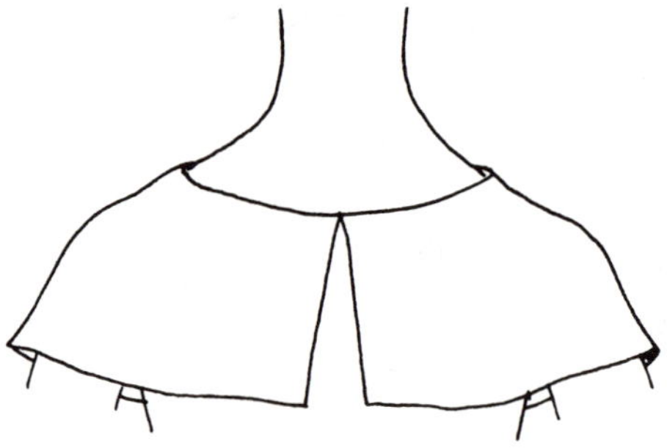

Cape
Collar

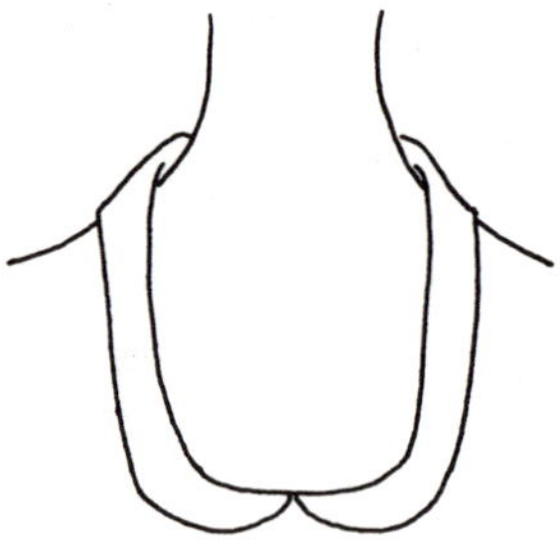

Bias-fold
Collar

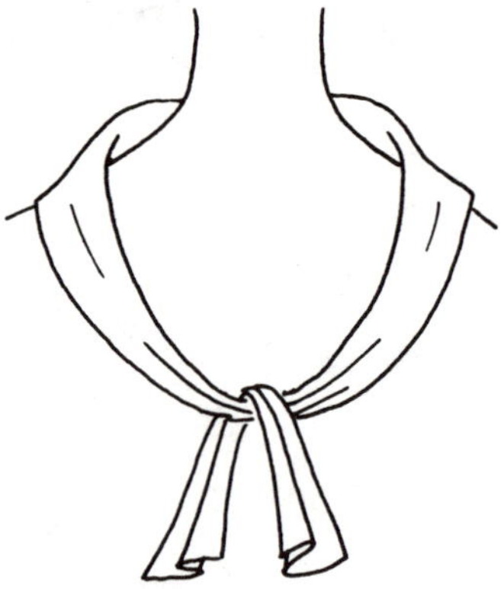

Tie-roll
Collar

LESSON TWENTY-SEVEN

designing variations on collars

By changing the size or shape of a basic collar, or through the addition of trimming, an unlimited number of interesting variations may be designed.

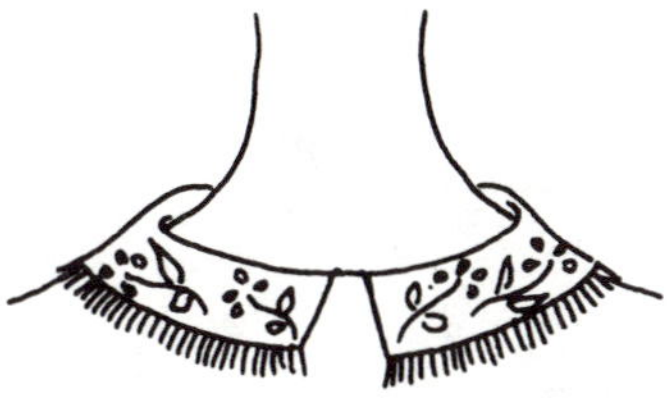

Peter Pan Collar Variation

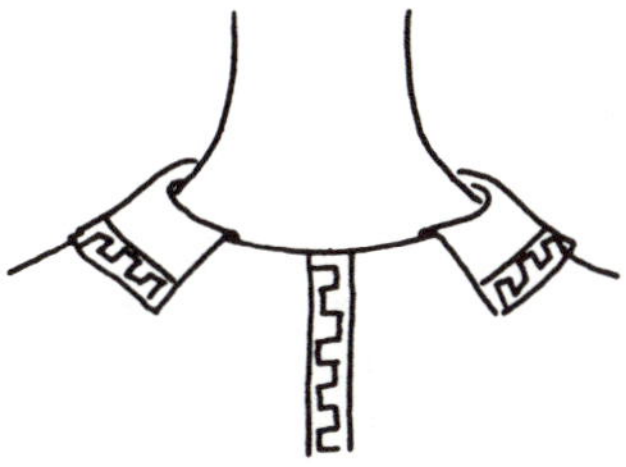

Spread Collar Variation

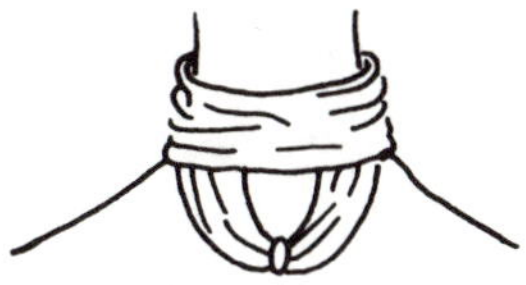

Clerical Collar Variation

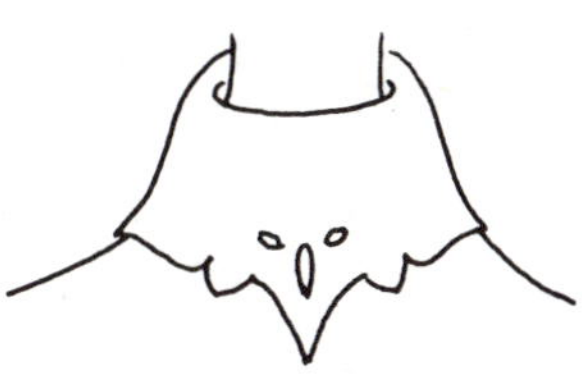

Turtleneck Collar Variation

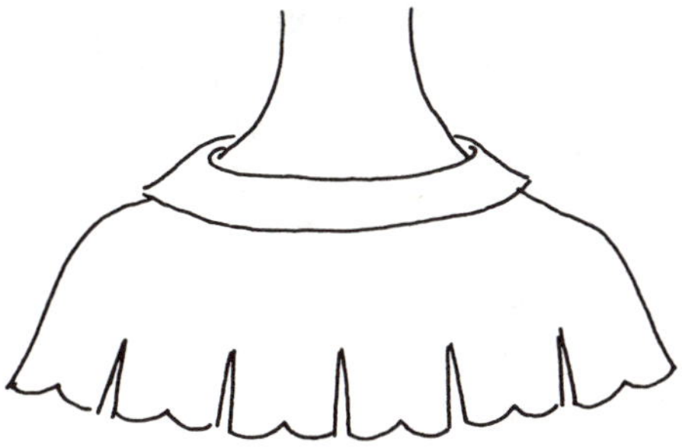

Bertha Collar Variation

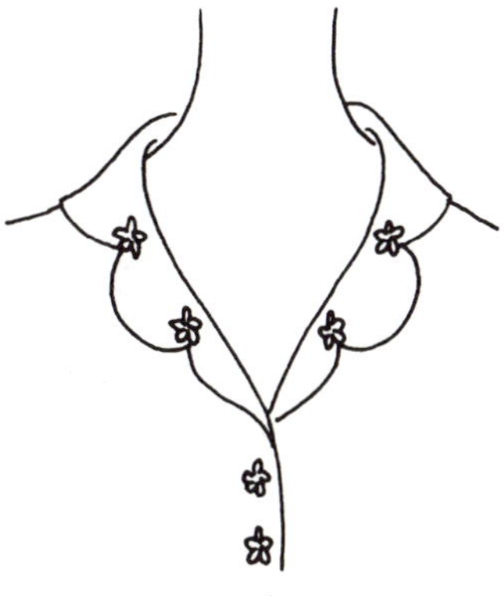

Notched Collar Variation

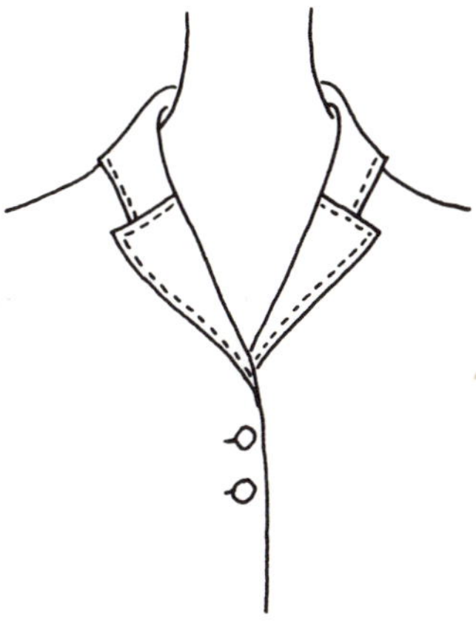

Convertible Collar Variation

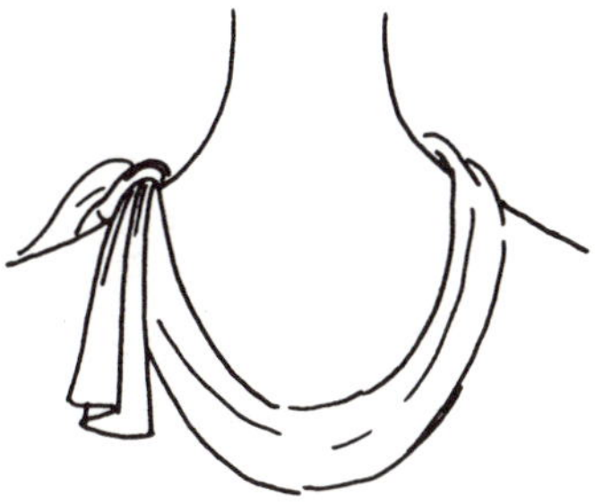

Tie-roll Collar Variation

EXERCISE 1

Figure 1 demonstrates the principle of drawing front-view collars. On tracing paper, over Figure 2, draw the Peter Pan, turtleneck, clerical, shawl, notched, and bias-fold collars. Finish with an accented line.

Correct your drawings by comparing them with those on pages 105 and 106.

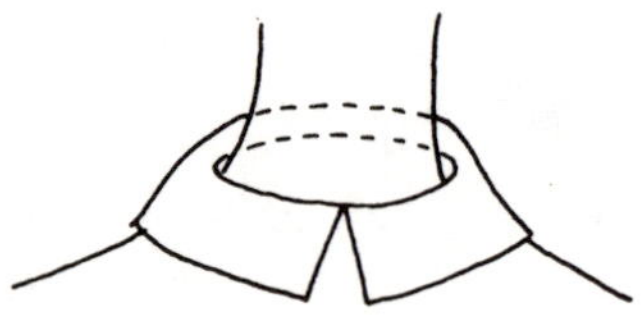

Figure 1

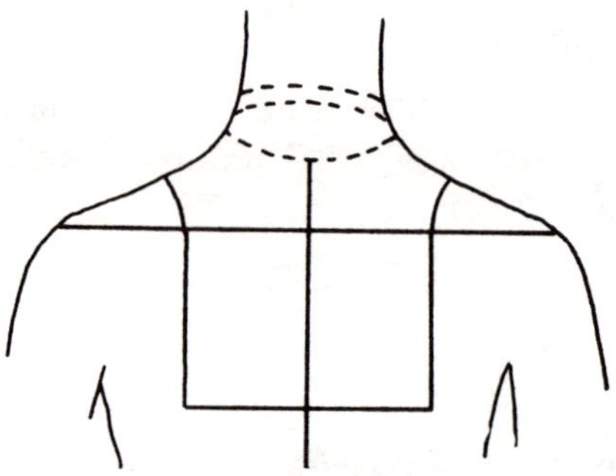

Figure 2

EXERCISE 2

On tracing paper, over a front-view croqui, design a variation for each basic collar. Select the ten best, and illustrate them on a sheet of vellum, using a complete coloring technique.

UNIT 16 basic sleeves

LESSON TWENTY-EIGHT

basic sleeves

A dress pattern may be constructed by drafting changes in the basic slopers (see page 35). In the same manner, all the basic sleeves and their many variations are derived from changes drafted in the basic sleeve sloper.

Sleeves generally fall into two categories: those which are "set in" to an armhole; and those which are partly or entirely an extension of the top portion of a garment, such as the raglan and kimono sleeves. Most set-in sleeves are sewn into a standard size armhole, but in the case of a casual sleeve, such as the roll-up, the normal armhole is lowered.

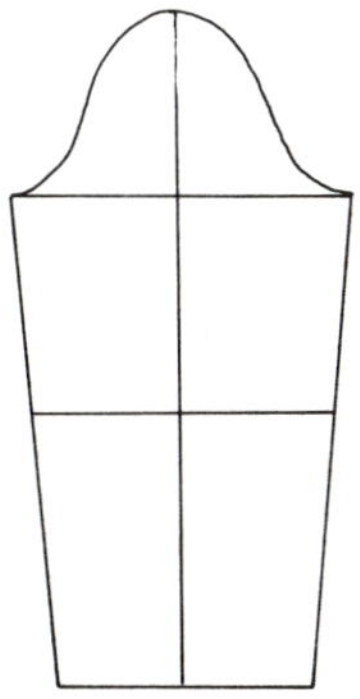

Basic Sleeve Sloper

Set-in Sleeves

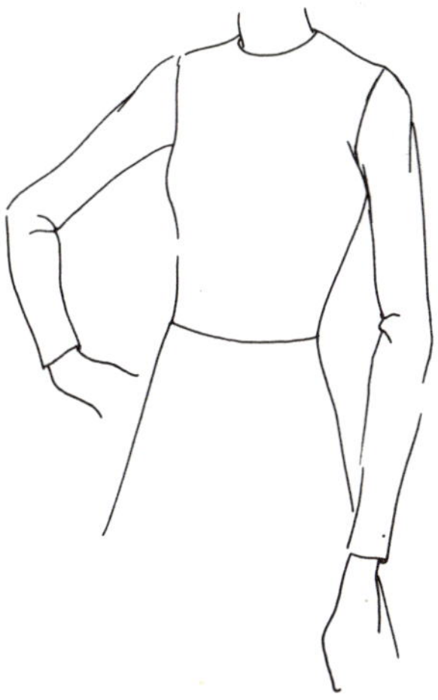

Set-in Bracelet Length Sleeve

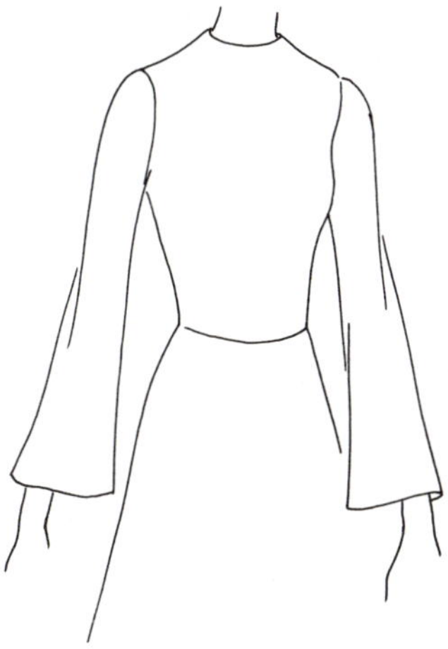

Bell Sleeve

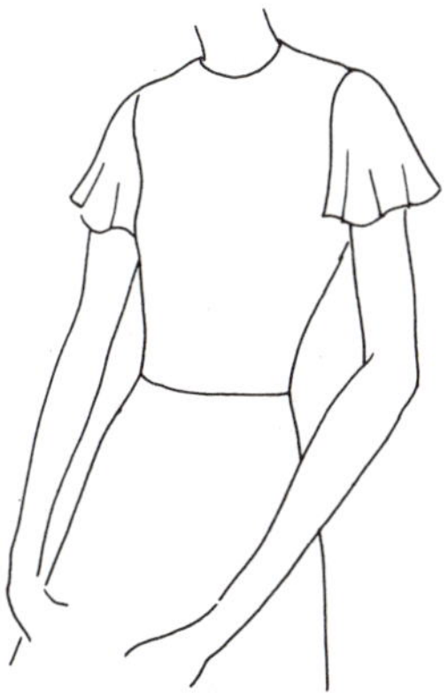

Cape Sleeve

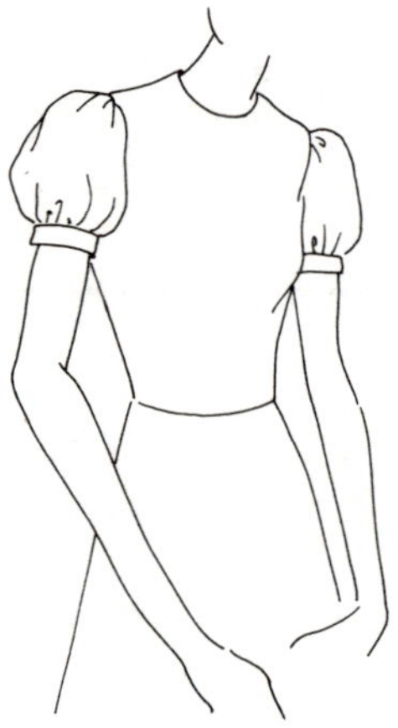

Short Puffed
Sleeve

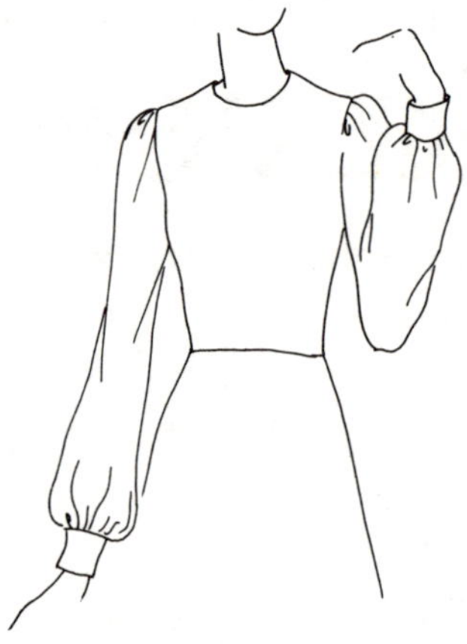

Long Puffed
Sleeve

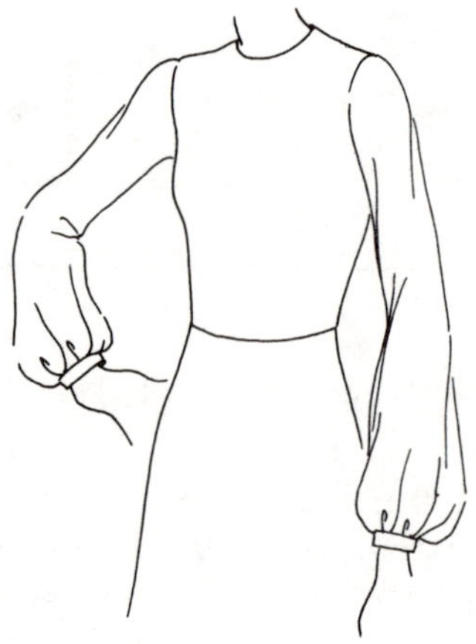

Bishop Sleeve

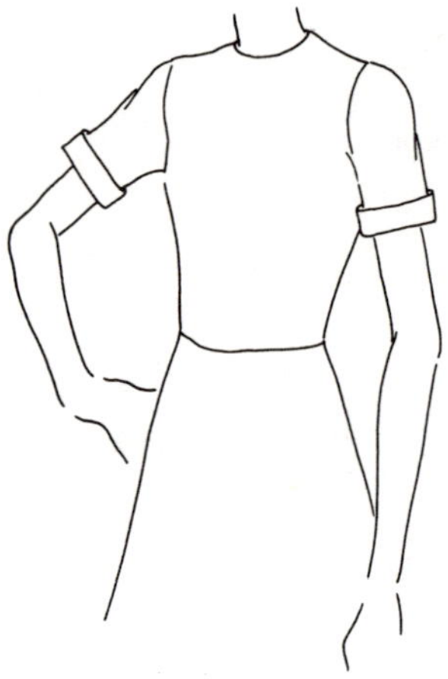

Roll-up Sleeve

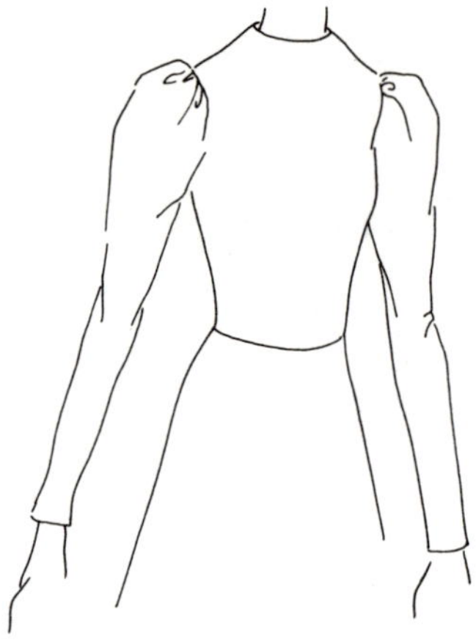

Leg-of-Mutton
Sleeve

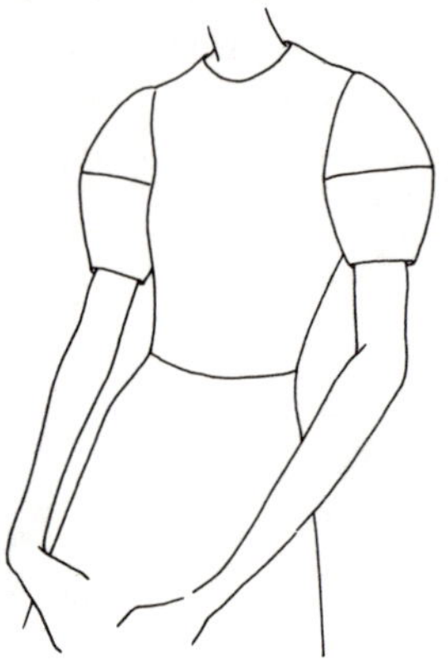

Lantern Sleeve

Sleeves Cut Partly or Entirely with the Top of A Garment

Cap Sleeve

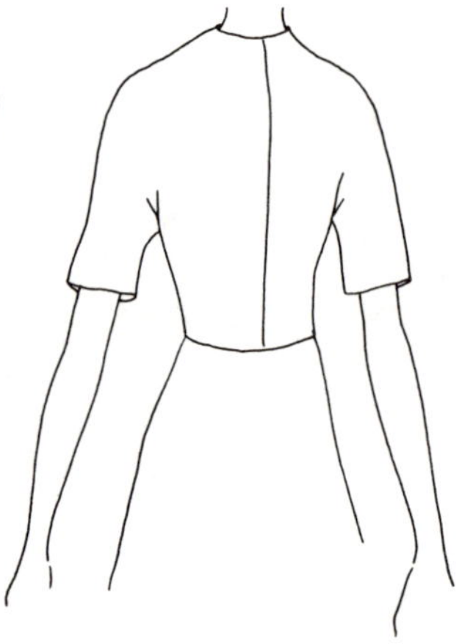

Kimono Sleeve

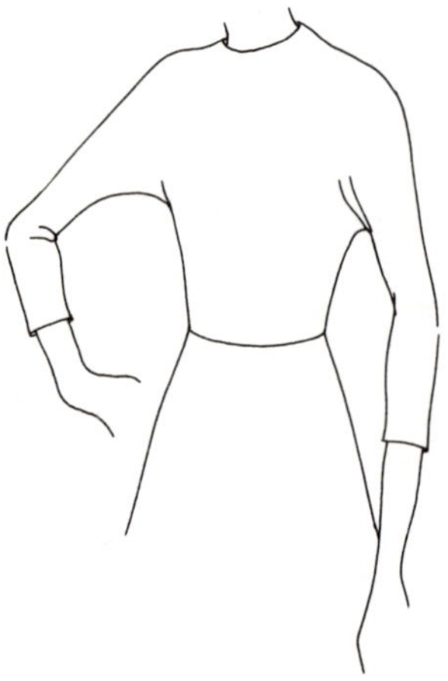

Dolman Sleeve

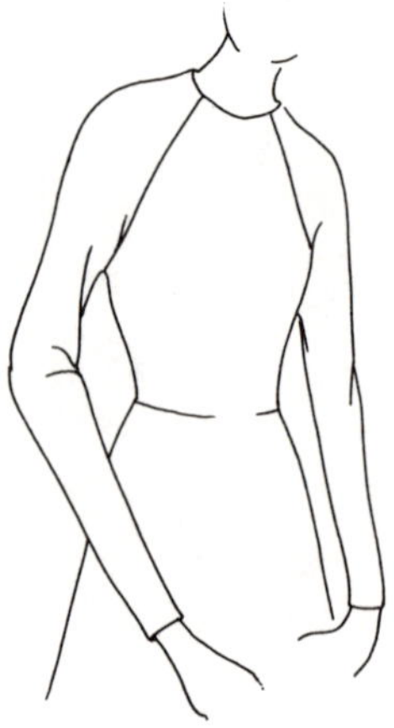

Raglan Sleeve

LESSON TWENTY-NINE

designing sleeve variations

Changing the silhouette of a basic sleeve creates a certain degree of variation. Trimming, seaming, stitching, pleating, and other design motifs may be employed to further the amount of variation desired.

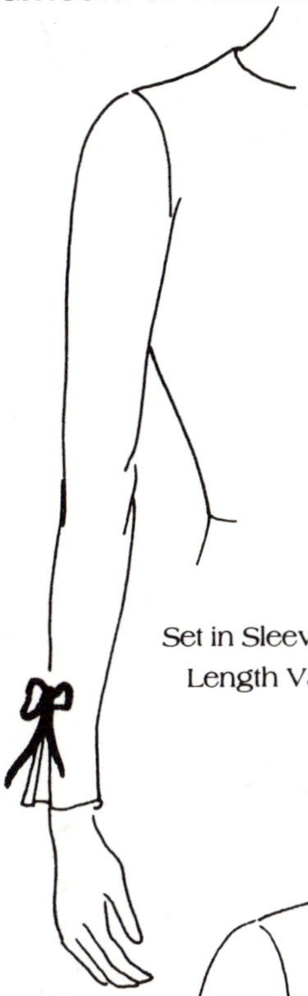

Set in Sleeve Bracelet Length Variation

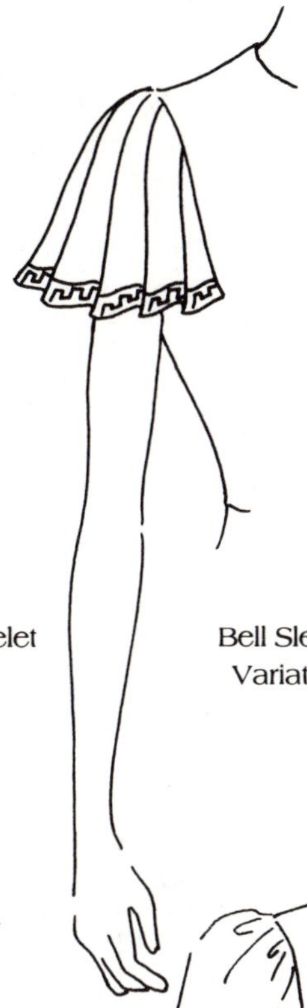

Bell Sleeve Variation

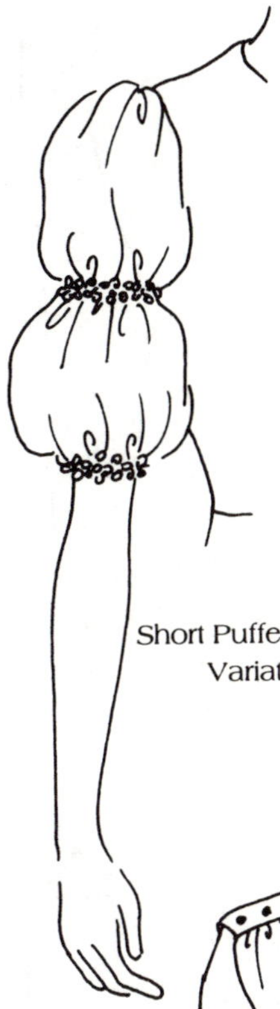

Short Puffed Sleeve Variation

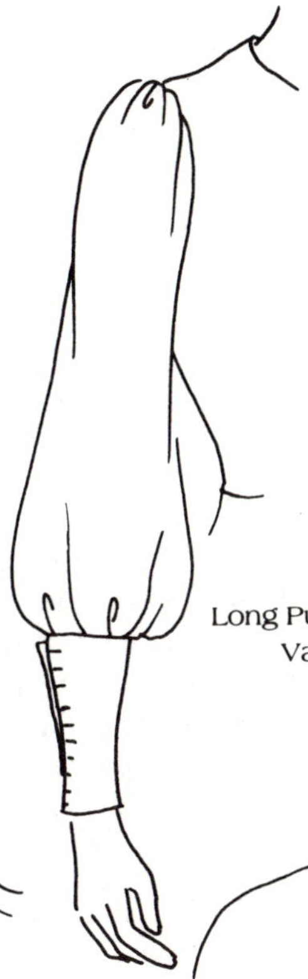

Long Puffed Sleeve Variation

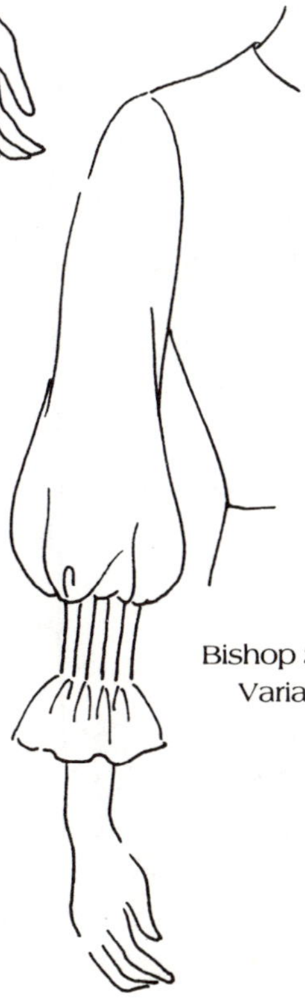

Bishop Sleeve Variation

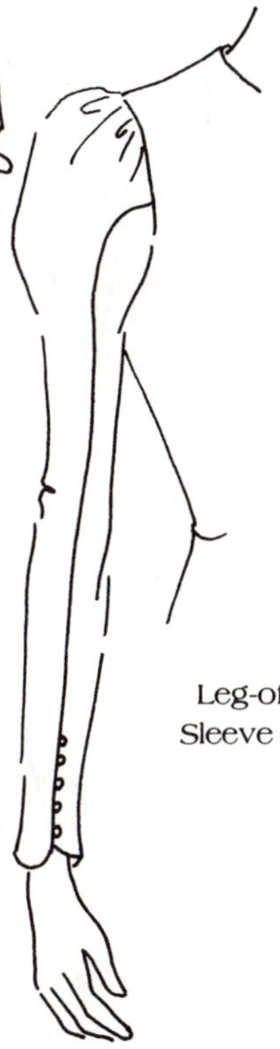

Leg-of-Mutton Sleeve Variation

Cap Sleeve Variation

Kimono Sleeve Variation

EXERCISE 1

On tracing paper, over the sleeve croqui on this page, draw all the basic sleeves. Correct your work by comparing it with the illustrations on pages 111 and 112.

EXERCISE 2

On tracing paper, over Figure 1, design two sleeve variations for each basic sleeve. Use a book on the history of costume as a source of inspiration. Select the ten best designs for illustration on vellum. Use either a complete or a partial coloring technique.

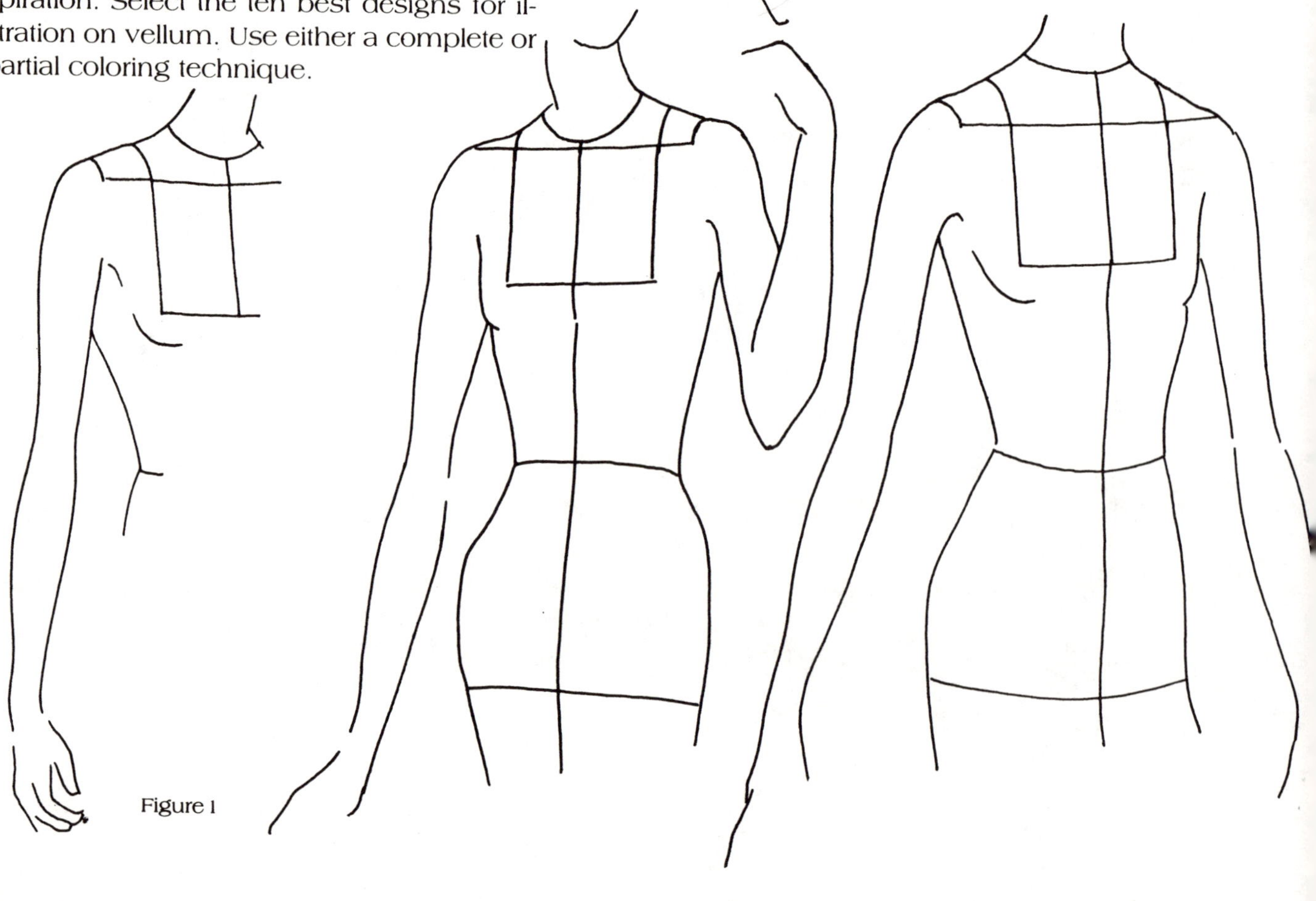

Figure 1

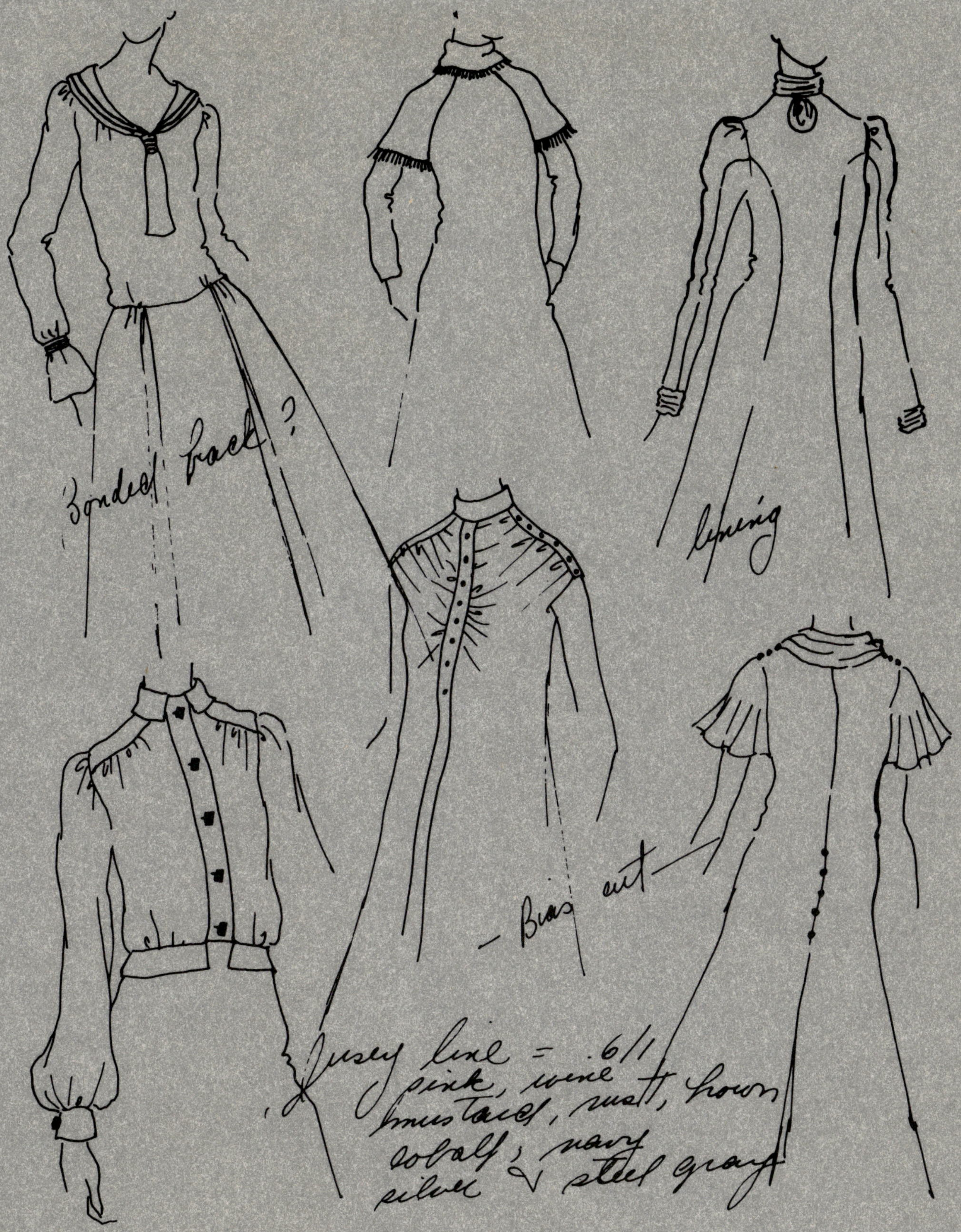
Bonded back?
lining
— Bias cut —
Jersey line = .6/1
pink, wine
mustard, rust, brown
cobalt, navy
silver & steel gray

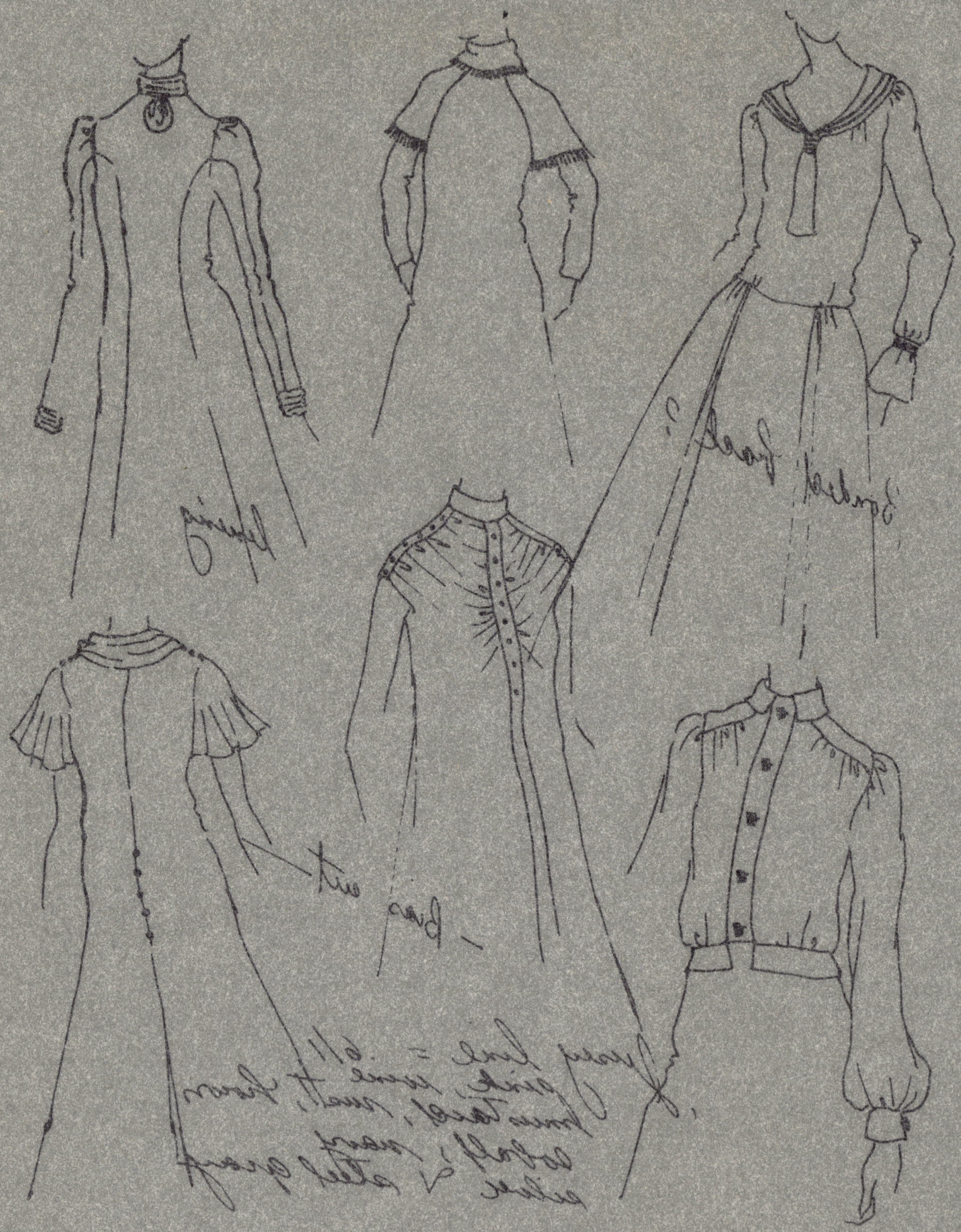

UNIT 17 designing for winter

LESSON THIRTY

a starting point

Every dress has a starting point. For some designers it is the silhouette; for others it may be a detail of trimming, a sleeve, a collar, an historical or a contemporary costume, the fabric from which a garment will be sewn, or any one of a number of other things.

The sketches on page 115, for example, seem to indicate that either collars or sleeves were probably the starting point for these designs, and that collar and sleeve coordination was a major theme.

PRACTICAL CONSIDERATIONS INFLUENCING DESIGNS

In addition to a starting point, or source of inspiration, practical considerations generally influence design. These considerations may include the following.

EXPENSE—A designer working for a manufacturer must consider "price line." The cost of manufacturing a garment is limited by the selling price; that is, the cost of production must be far enough below the selling price to allow a manufacturer a reasonable margin of profit. Since some apparel is more expensive to produce than others, the designer functions within a budget.

CLIMATE AND OCCASION—Dresses are designed for a time of year, a time of day or night, and certain kinds of activities. The thoughtful designer will consider physical comfort and the function of a garment, as well as expense.

AGE GROUP AND FIGURE SIZE—Age group and figure size are among the most crucial factors influencing design. Students of fashion often begin their careers with starry-eyed visions of the glamorous world of haute couture. But in a country such as the United States, with its greatest population falling in the middle class, and an increasing number of elderly and young people, only a small percentage of all the clothes designed and manufactured belongs to the world of high fashion.

The average designer works within a particular category, such as infants', toddlers', or children's wear; sub-teen and junior petite; junior and misses'; or women's and half sizes—and each one requires an approach to design completely different from the others.

LESSON THIRTY-ONE

exercises

EXERCISE 1

On tracing paper over a three-quarter-view croqui, design six winter daytime dresses. Use as a starting point for each design one of your original sleeve or collar variations. Try to coordinate collars, sleeves, and silhouettes.

EXERCISE 2

On the following pages are a selection of croquis for different age and size groups. Choose one group and design six early evening (cocktail or party hour) dresses appropriate for the group of your choice. Name the fabric.

EXERCISE 3

Select your three best designs. Illustrate on vellum, using a partial coloring technique.

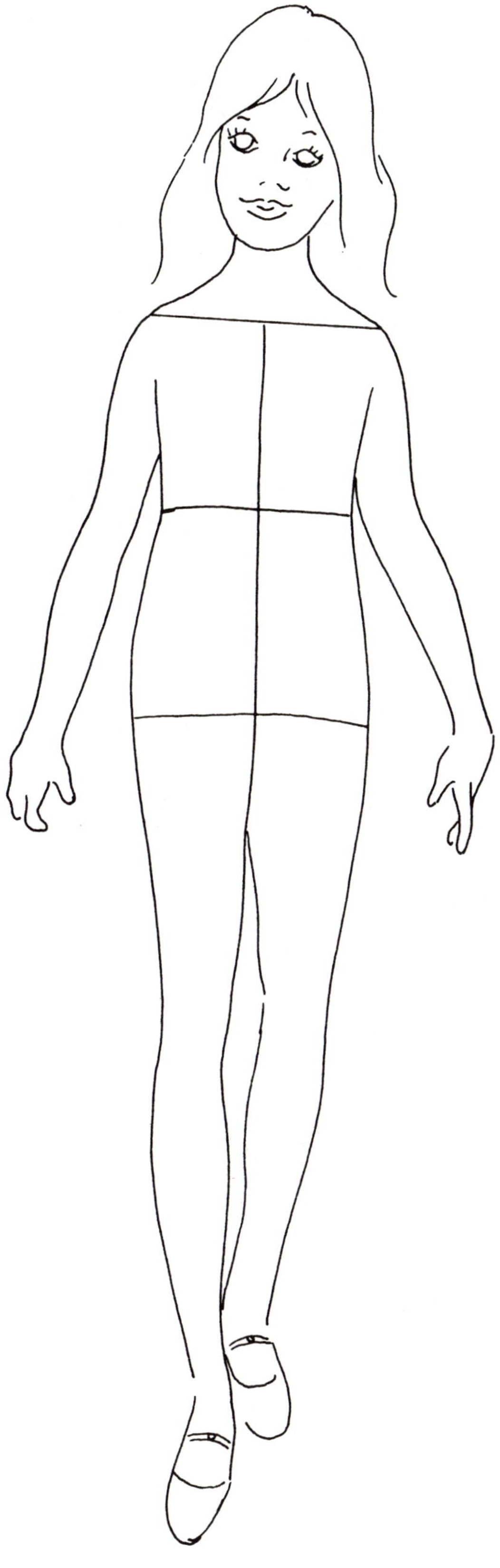

Figure 1. Children

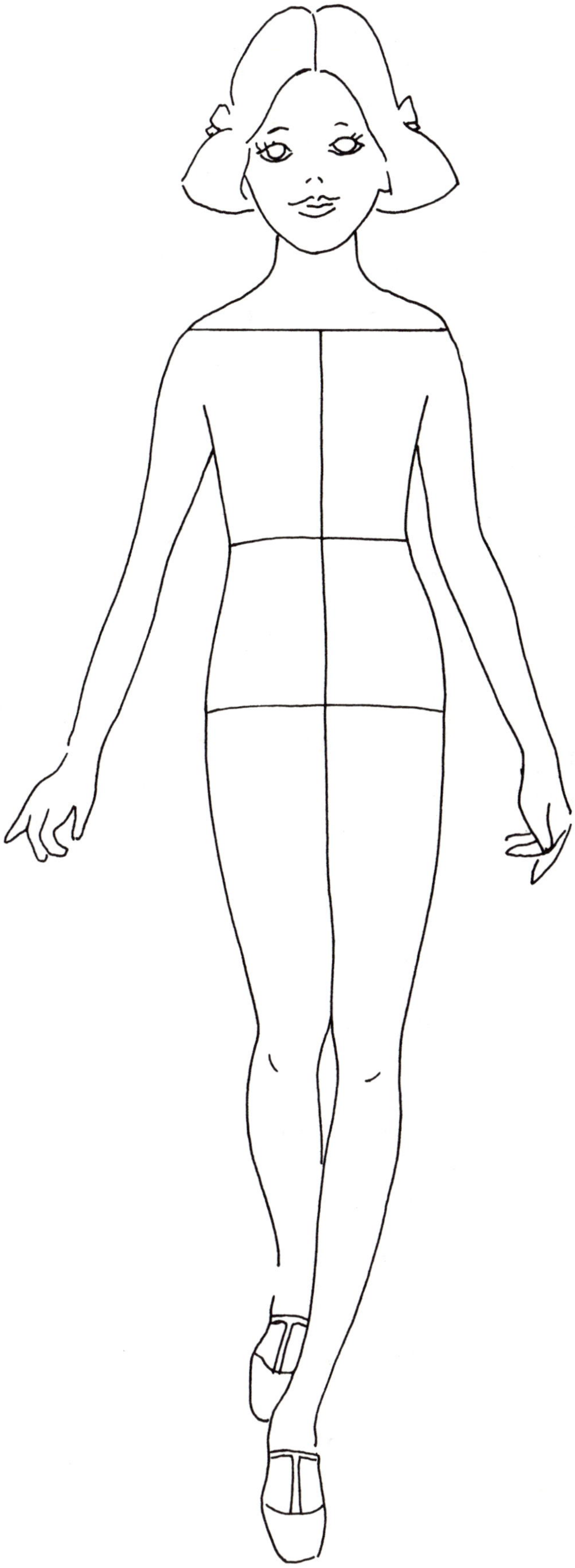

Figure 2. Children

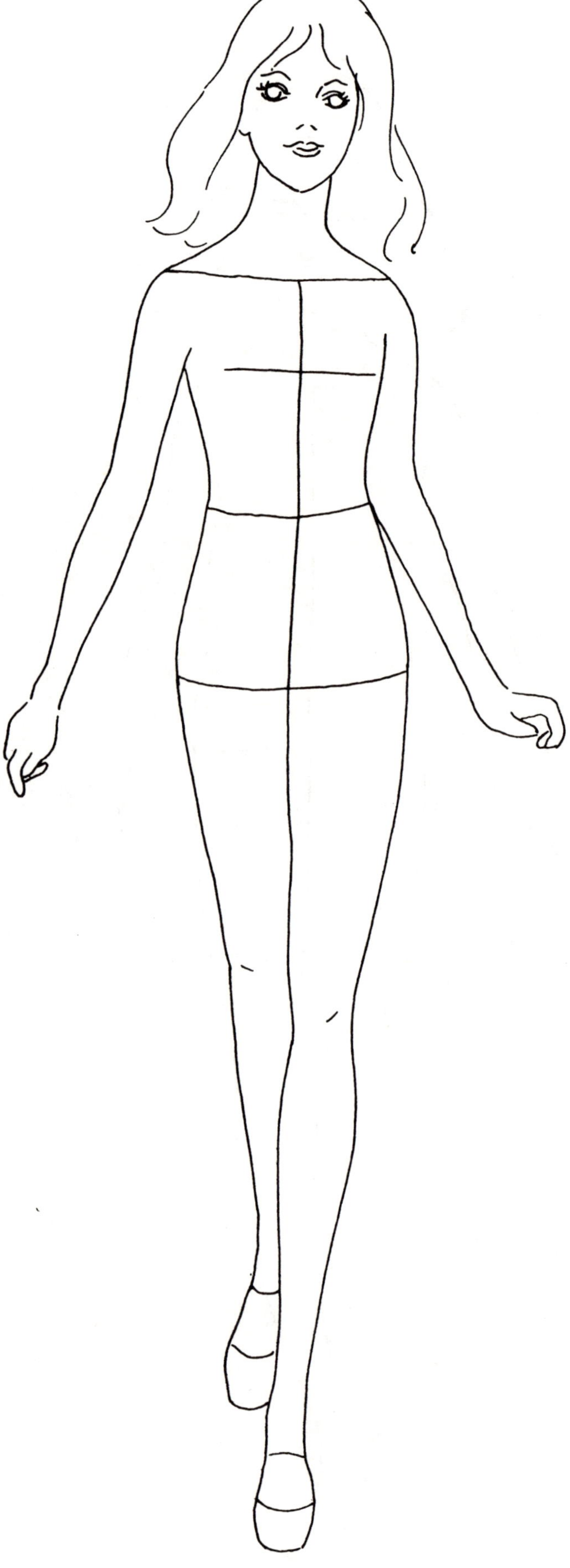

Figure 3. Junior Teen

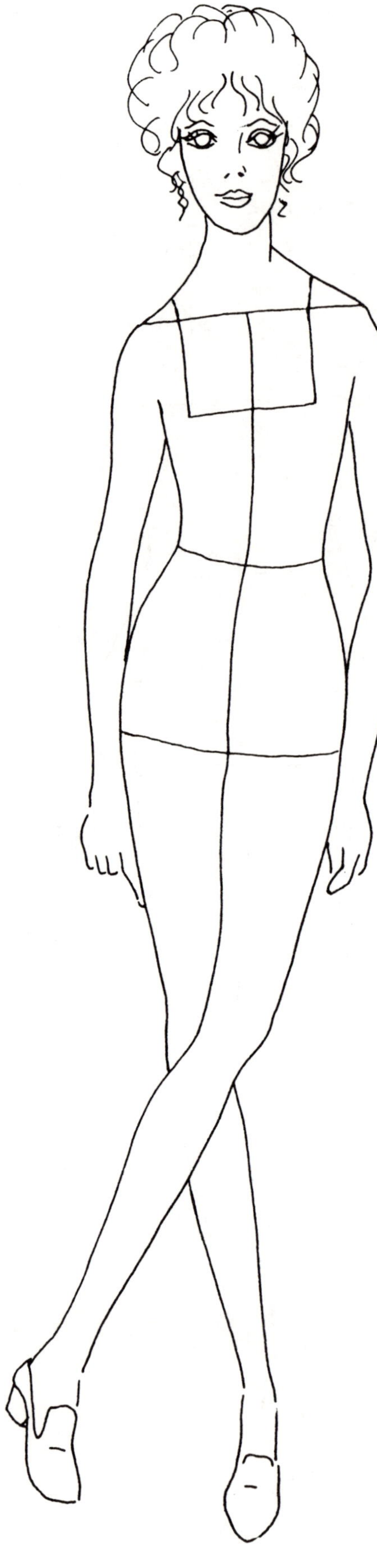

Figure 4. Junior Petite

Figure 5. Misses

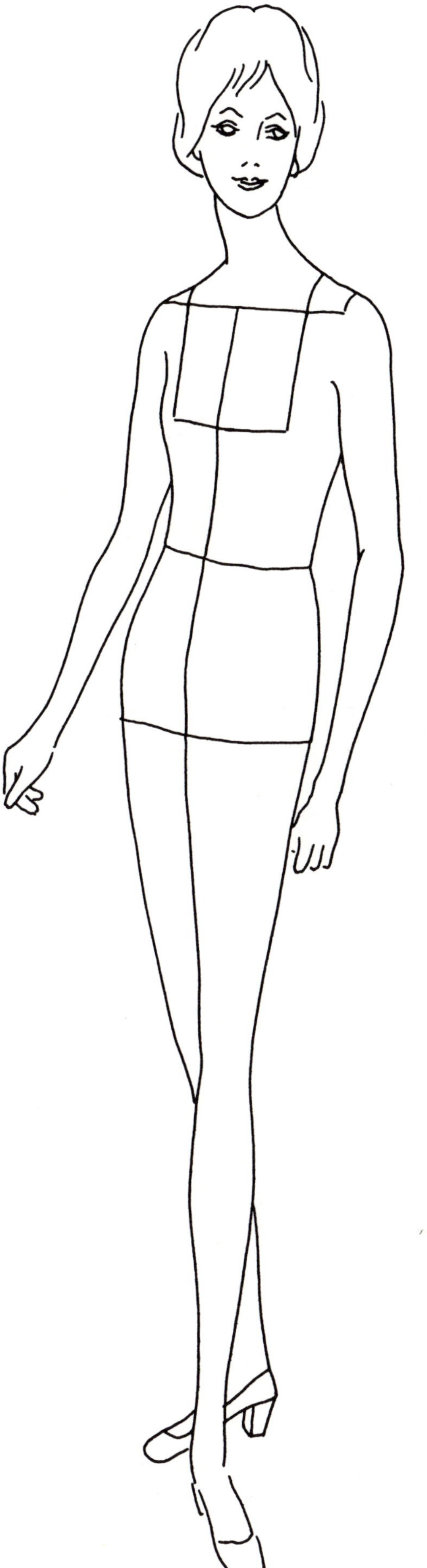

Figure 6. Women's